WITHDRAWN

Beowulf

Beowulf

A Translation and Commentary

Marc Hudson

Lewisburg
Bucknell University Press
London and Toronto: Associated University Presses

© 1990 by Associated University Presses, Inc.

All rights reserved. Authorization to photocopy items for internal or personal use, or the internal or personal use of specific clients, is granted by the copyright owner, provided that a base fee of $10.00, plus eight cents per page, per copy is paid directly to the Copyright Clearance Center, 27 Congress Street, Salem, Massachusetts 01970. [0–8383–5162–8/90 $10.00+8¢ pp, pc.]

Associated University Presses
440 Forsgate Drive
Cranbury, NJ 08512

Associated University Presses
25 Sicilian Avenue
London WC1A 2QH, England

Associated University Presses
P.O. Box 488, Port Credit
Mississauga, Ontario
Canada L5G 4M2

The paper used in this publication meets the requirements of the American National Standard for Permanence of Paper for Printed Library Materials Z39.48–1984.

Library of Congress Cataloging-in-Publication Data

Hudson, Marc, 1947–
  Beowulf : a translation and commentary / Marc Hudson.
    p.   cm.
  Includes bibliographical references.
  ISBN 0-8387-5162-8 (alk. paper)
  1. Beowulf.   2. Epic poetry, English (Old)—History and criticism.
3. Epic poetry, English (Old)—Modernized versions.   I. Beowulf.
II. Title.
PR1585.H84   1990
829'.3—dc20   88-43407
                                                                              CIP

PRINTED IN THE UNITED STATES OF AMERICA

for Robert D. Stevick

Contents

Acknowledgments 9

Part 1. Commentary

1 On the Translation of *Beowulf* 15
2 Choosing the Form 25
3 Diction 35
4 The Syntax of Contemplation 48
5 The Act of Translation 61
Notes 84

Part 2. A Translation of Beowulf

Beowulf 95
Selected Sources 171

Acknowledgments

A translator always acquires debts he or she cannot repay. The whole enterprise leans against the scholars who have compiled the dictionaries, edited the manuscripts, written the critical commentaries. I lived so long with Klaeber at my elbow that that compact edition of *Beowulf* in its binding of brown cloth will always seem an amiable colleague. Here I have not the space to recognize many whose work has been essential for my own, including the several translators whose efforts I evaluate in my commentary. Scholars and fellow translators, we are all part of that sedentary comitatus devoted to the poem. Let me here acknowledge my debt to all those whose work I cite.

But now it is my pleasure to recognize those who have given me more direct encouragement and assistance. First, I must thank Professor Robert Stevick of the University of Washington, whose *Beowulf* course in the spring of 1979 was my introduction to the poem in its original language. His large and generous vision of *Beowulf* was indeed the instrumental cause of this present work. In the ensuing years, he gave me much patient encouragement and counsel. In dedicating this book to him, I acknowledge my gratitude for his superb teaching. His colleague, Professor David Fowler, read much of the translation and offered many valuable suggestions. Later, Professor Miceal Vaughan, Professor Sally Mussetter, and Professor William Matthews read the entire manuscript and made many discerning and helpful criticisms. I also must thank Janie Johnson, who typed the original manuscript; Elizabeth Tsutakawa, who later typed and corrected the translation, an unlooked-for kindness; and Debbie Wagers, who typed the final version of the notes and the bibliography. I also owe much to my friend, Eric Dahl, who encouraged me to believe that the translation had merit. And, finally, to my dearest friend and wife, the Old Norse scholar, Helen Mundy Hudson, who has listened to many of the lines as I worked on them: I could always test them against her intuitive intelligence. She read the commentary and made many suggestions that I incorporated into my various revisions. Throughout, she has encouraged me and given me good counsel, helping me to remain mindful of the translator's first debt, the one, if he is lucky, he can partly discharge, that to the genius of the work he serves.

Permission has been granted for the following:
Excerpts from *Beowulf: A Verse Translation* by Michael Alexander, copyright © 1973 by Michael Alexander, have been reprinted by permission of Penguin Books. Excerpts from *Beowulf*, translated by Howell D. Chickering, Jr. Copyright © 1977 by Howell D. Chickering, Jr. Reprinted by permission of Doubleday, a division on Bantam, Doubleday, Dell Publishing Group, Inc. Excerpts from *Beowulf*, translated by Kevin Crossley-Holland. Translation copyright © 1968 by Kevin Crossley-Holland. Reprinted by permission of Farrar, Straus and Giroux, Inc. Excerpts from *Beowulf: The Oldest English Epic*, translated by Charles W. Kennedy, and *Collected Poems 1930–1986* by Richard Eberhart. Reprinted by permission of Oxford University Press. Excerpts from *Beowulf*, edited by Fr. Klaeber, have been reprinted by permission of D. C. Heath and Company. Excerpts from *Beowulf*, translated by Edwin Morgan, reprinted by permission of Edwin Morgan. Excerpts from *Beowulf*, translated by Burton Raffel (Amherst: University of Massachusetts Press, 1971), copyright © 1971 by the University of Massachusetts Press and reprinted by permission. Excerpts from *Beowulf*, translated by Mary Waterhouse, have been reprinted by permission of The Bodley Head Limited. Excerpts from *The Finn Episode in Beowulf* by R. A. Williams have been reprinted by permission of Cambridge University Press. Excerpts from *A Choice of Anglo-Saxon Verse*, translated by Richard Hamer, are reprinted by permission of Faber and Faber Limited. Excerpts from *Tree and Leaf* by J. R. R. Tolkien are reprinted by permission of Unwin Hyman Ltd. Lines from "A Coat" by William Butler Yeats reprinted with permission of Macmillan Publishing Company from *Collected Poems* by William Butler Yeats. Copyright 1916 by Macmillan Publishing Company, renewed 1944 by Bertha Georgie Yeats. Lines from "My Table" by William Butler Yeats reprinted with permission of Macmillan Publishing Company from *Collected Poems* by William Butler Yeats. Copyright 1928 by Macmillan Publishing Company, renewed 1956 by Georgie Yeats. Excerpt from "Burnt Norton" in *Four Quartets*, copyright 1943 by T. S. Eliot and renewed 1971 by Esme Valerie Eliot, reprinted with permission of Harcourt Brace Jovanovich, Inc.

Beowulf

Part 1
Commentary

1
On the Translation of *Beowulf*

To read in the large literature on the theory of translation is somewhat like overhearing the melancholy conversation of the survivors of shipwreck. The ship has gone down and with it a cargo of wine, vellum, and beeswax. The question asked is, "How many survivors?" The most pessimistic would answer, "At best a handful. And the poor merchant is a ruined man—not one of the three thousand amphorae was salvaged." There would speak a Nabokov. Yet another, much more sanguine, a Jackson Mathews, might reply, "Only the captain was lost. All the rest—crew, passengers, the captain's wife, even her lapdog—all survived, though of necessity they underwent a sea change. And the very waves that wrecked us have miraculously brought to shore the bulk of the cargo."

Critics agree that loss in translation is inevitable; the measure of loss is keenly debated. Faithful translation, Nabokov believes, is an oxymoron; and so he counsels the most servile sort of metaphrase, a line-by-line literal transcription, copiously annotated.[1] Yet the consensus is that the best translation gives the effect of passing effortlessly from language to language, as through a permeable membrane, achieving a faithful version of the original.

I did write "version." Transformation, as well as loss, is inevitable. And so we "may compare the work of a translator with that of an artist who is asked to create an exact replica of a marble statue, but who cannot secure any marble."[2] However great the copyist's gifts, and however excellent the material that he uses, his work can never replicate the original. Each language has its own properties, and the translator must become a dealer in equivalences rather than exactitudes.

This is no less true of the relationship between Old English and Modern English, despite their kinship, the haunting echoes of cognates, and collocations like "ham and heorð" (home and hearth). The infusion of French and Latin words during the later Middle Ages and the Renaissance softened, and mellowed somewhat, the

Germanic hardness. The loss of inflection loosened the regimen of the syntax and spawned those "little words"—prepositions and articles—that have reduced the density of the English language. For these reasons, Modern English does seem to be a softer medium—applewood, say, compared to oak—neither quite so intractable nor so unyielding as Old English. It is capable of a more fluid, a more mellifluous line. Conversely, it is difficult to secure in Modern English the crabbed tenseness and the ridgelike accents that give the old poetry its stern character.

The translator of Old English is faced with all the same potential for betrayal as any translator; and at the outset, he must make the old choice about how freehanded, or conservative, a *traduttore* he will be. Dryden still seems to have best formulated the translator's possible approaches to his task:

> All Translation I suppose may be reduced to these three heads:
> First, that of Metaphrase, or turning an Authour word by word and Line by Line, from one Language into another. . . . The second way is that of Paraphrase, or Translation with Latitude, where the Authour is kept in view by the Translator, so as never to be lost, but his words are not so strictly follow'd as his sense, and that too is admitted to be amplyfied, but not alter'd. . . . The Third way is that of Imitation, where the Translator (if now he has not lost that Name) assumes the liberty not only to vary from the words and sence, but to forsake them both as he sees occasion: and taking only some general hints from the Original, to run division on the ground-work, as he pleases.[3]

Good Augustan that he was, Dryden argued brilliantly for the middle way of paraphrase. He compares the act of metaphrasing to that of a man "dancing on Ropes with fetter'd Leggs."[4] Attempting to be too faithful to the word, the translator may lose the spirit and so produce a corpse, and a handcuffed and hobbled one at that.

The imitator risks the other limit—he gives his own energies as a poet such free play that he breaks his ties with the original, using it only as inspiration, like a composer stealing a motif and elaborating it so successfully that the first owner is dispossessed of it. Beautiful music may result, but it is not translation. Dryden concludes: "To state it fairly, Imitation of an Authour is the most advantagious way for a Translator to shew himself, but the greatest wrong which can be done to the Memory and Reputation of the dead."[5] With this caveat: a poet like Pindar who is "generally known to be a dark writer, to want Connexion, (I mean as to our understanding), to soar out of sight, and leave his Reader at a

Gaze ... cannot be Translated literally."⁶ Only such a poet as Abraham Cowley could "make Pindar speak *English,* and that was to be perform'd by no other way than Imitation."⁷

Arguably, the *Beowulf* poet is a "dark writer." Though one suspects he was readily comprehensible to his medieval audience, he often leaves his twentieth-century reader at a gaze, and doubly so when nodding scribes in collusion with the ravages of time have botched the manuscript. Here the translator-imitator may find justification for his liberties. But, obviously, to travel on this path with any success the translator must be a good poet in his own right.

The bias of translators in our own century has been toward imitation. Following the powerful influence of Pound and his work with the medieval Provençal poets, Cavalcanti, and the Chinese poets, many of our finest translators have worked in this vein.⁸ Unlike Dryden, I would not dismiss these efforts out of hand as merely exercises for translators to show themselves to advantage at the expense of the dead. Pound and many others have revealed that fidelity can sometimes be achieved through what some would consider a licentious freedom.

Paraphrase, however, is the path that Dryden endorses. Even the great Anglo-Saxon translator King Alfred of Wessex apparently anticipated the validity of Dryden's preference. Although he wrote in his Preface to the *Cura Pastoralis* that he translated "hwilum word be worde, hwilum andgit of andgite" ("sometimes word by word, sometimes meaning by meaning"), he seemed to favor paraphrase in his practice.⁹ In paraphrase, the translator's freedom is limited by the discipline of fidelity to the original text's meaning. He does not enjoy the godlike liberty of the imitator, nor does he suffer the convictlike servitude of the metaphraser. He is neither his own man, nor his author's myrmidon; he is rather like the good Christian, a creature with a free will and yet a servant to the Logos.

Liberal paraphrase might describe the path I took, and in the subsequent chapters I will discuss the choices I made in form, diction, imagery, and syntax following that path. Translation, like all the arts, is inevitably provisional and impressionistic. Theory can lead only a short distance into the wood and give a general instrument for finding the way; the rest is up to the translator's *prudentia* and *ars*—the shrewdness of his ability to interpret the old poem and his skills as a writer in his native language. He proceeds "word by word, meaning by meaning," making provisional readings, provisional versions, learning as he goes when to relax and when to look sharp, muttering repeatedly to himself, "this is not good enough," even of those lines which came to him as a certain gift and by which he would stand until the crack of doom. That is, he must be dogged by a sense of failure, for only then has he the least chance of succeeding, of finding, as Walter Benjamin expresses it, "that latent structure which can awaken an echo of the original."[10]

Metaphrase, paraphrase, imitation—as useful as the model has proved in thinking about translation, George Steiner in *After Babel* finds the classification shopworn. He would pose instead a fourfold hermeneutic motion that encompasses the translator's "act of elicitation and appropriative transfer of meaning."[11] An exploration of Steiner's model should illumine and broaden the base of our discussion.

First, there is an "initiative trust, an investment of belief . . . in the meaningfulness, the 'seriousness' of the facing or, strictly speaking, adverse text."[12] A poem of *Beowulf*'s stature can be granted this trust with little difficulty.

"After trust," writes Steiner, "comes aggression. . . . The translator invades, extracts, and brings home."[13] Philemon Holland, the Elizabethan translator of Xenophon and Pliny, "looked on his achievements as conquests, and so described them."[14] Saint Jerome wrote of meaning "brought home captive by the translator."[15] To use a Saxon-like metaphor, we plunder the foreign word-hoard, do violence to, even when we do not betray, the original artifact. This aggression, however, is balanced by compensation, which we will examine in a moment.

"The third movement," Steiner goes on, "is incorporative: The import, of meaning and of form, the embodiment, is not made in or into a vacuum."[16] A translation may or may not be at home in the to-language. Compare, for instance, the strangeness of Morris's archaic translation of *Beowulf* to the at-homeness of North's Elizabethan translation of Plutarch. One is a prodigy without issue; the other helped sire some of Shakespeare's greatest plays. For the translator of *Beowulf*, consideration of this movement raises the perplexing question of diction. The revolution in poetics of the past eighty years, demolishing all vestiges of an inherited poetic language, makes the translation of a poem constructed, at least partly, of inherited formulas a problematical task.

Finally, "the hermeneutic act must compensate. If it is to be authentic, it must mediate into exchange and restored parity."[17] Steiner considers this movement at the core of the ethics of translation: the new work must cast some luster back on the original, dignify it, and adumbrate its meaning.[18] Each of the translations of *Beowulf* offers a variant reading. There is Donaldson's with its emphasis on the contrast between the poem's "rhetorical elaboration" and its "barest simplicity of statement;"[19] Raffel's with its passion for the "poetry" of the original; Morgan's with its attentiveness to the form of the original. Each is a different mirror, illumining various aspects of the poem. Steiner observes that the translator's gift back to the poem may consist of his failures: "The failings of the translator . . . localize . . . the resistant vitalities, the opaque centres of specific genius in the original."[20] In the instance of Old English verse, what has been called "interlace structure"[21] is one of those "resistant vitalities." A translator must wrench the structure of his own language to be faithful to the syntax of Old English poems.

In such ways, then, the translator illumines, clarifies, even fulfills meanings latent in the original; in certain instances, he may surpass the original, inferring "that the source text possesses potentialities, elemental reserves as yet unrealized by itself."[22]

Steiner does believe in the possibility of good translation, however seldom achieved. He refers the reader to Donne's "Extasie" and the thesis "that there occurs in the spiritual and carnal union of authentic love a commingling, an osmotic confluence of two souls," an "interanimation."[23] Love, then, is the paradigm of true translation:

> "Interanimation" signifies a process of totally attentive interpenetration. It tells of a dialectic of fusion in which identity survives altered but also strengthened and redefined by virtue of reciprocity. There is annihilation of self in the other consciousness and recognition of self in a mirroring motion. Principally, there results a multiplication of resource, of affirmed being.[24]

To achieve this interanimation, Steiner hypothesizes an almost mystical state of receptivity on the part of the translator, recalling Keats's twilit identification with the nightingale and Rilke's clairvoyant fortnight as an amanuensis to the angelic voices at Duino. As Wilamowitz wrote, "True translation is metempsychosis."[25]

Metempsychosis served Valéry when he undertook the translation of Virgil's *Eclogues*, imagining "the moment of composition, the 'still fluid state' of mind of the young Virgil."[26] But is such a technique of imaginative recreation at all possible for the translator of *Beowulf*? Virgil is a thousand years more remote from us than the *Beowulf* poet, but he is much closer to us culturally; Pope and Dryden dealt with him as a fellow Augustan. Saxon York is far more alien to us than classical Rome. Conceivably, a poet could retrieve enough of the cultural context of the *Eclogues* to intuit Virgil's state of mind when he wrote them. But can the translator of *Beowulf* reach back into the mind of that seventh, or eighth, or eleventh century Mercian, or Northumbrian, or East Anglian scop or priest? Indeed, our poet has become his poem. The closest readers come to his signature is in those compounds and kennings that are the clearest index of his genius. These are the only tracks the poet has left us.

As if this were not difficulty enough, the condition of the manuscript itself presents a barrier to the clairvoyant would-be translator: in addition to the leaves scorched by the Cottonian fire of 1731, letters have faded to the point of illegibility. Folio 182, containing the dragon fight, is quite worn out—presumably because it was so avidly fingered and read. Worn, fire-scorched, sparsely punctuated, ridden with scribal errors, the poem exists only in conjectural modern transcriptions.

While these uncertainties cast suspicion on the entire translation process, they are not the translator's chief headache. Dorothy Whitelock, the scholar who has perhaps shed the most light on the poem, has revealed most fully how dark the poem is to us. She reminds us just how much the poem's original audience knew that we do not. For instance, Whitelock argues that the poet would not have followed the tale of Finn with the aside that peace did not reign in the Danish court forever unless he expected his audience to remember that Hrothulf killed Hrethric. For a similar effect, Whitelock contends, the poet mentions Heoroweard's name:

> So, towards the end of the first part of the poem . . . he [the poet] has only to mention Heoroweard's name—and he goes out of his way to do so—and the whole of the final act of the Scylding drama would leap into his audience's minds, one of the most famous events in northern story, which gave rise to the Old Norse poem, the *Bjarkamál*, namely the slaying of Hrothulf by his cousin Heoroweard.[27]

Whitelock's point is that the poet collaborates with his audience's memory: he need only mention a name and an entire legend springs to mind and a pattern is fulfilled. By such allusions the poem becomes an epic, bodying forth a people's cosmogony and mythos. Yet Whitelock's earlier phrase—"To an audience that did not know that Hrothulf killed Hrethric, the whole section would be pointless"[28]—echoes sternly. "We can reasonably suspect,"

Shippey writes, "the poet and his audience felt 'continuity,' if not identity, with dead heroes."[29] The translator and his audience assuredly do not. Unless we are scholars of Old Norse as well as of Old English, the allusion to Heoroweard falls on deaf ears. The story is recorded in Saxo Grammaticus's version of the *Bjarkamál*, but what if, with the usual ravages of time, it had perished by moth or fire? Even a critic as skilled as Dorothy Whitelock could only have lifted a puzzled eyebrow, and passed on, with that feeling which must be akin to that of an amnesia victim, encountering some memento of her earlier life. It is a question of memory, most of which is irrecoverably lost. If his intended audience is not the Old English scholar, the translator of *Beowulf* can count on virtually no collaboration with his reader's memory.

It may be said, then, that *Beowulf* is a fragment. The poem is embedded in a matrix—a time and a tradition—alien to us. Its full meaning depends on the extraliterary frame, from the deciphering of maxims to the determination of colors, from the proper description of heroic equipage to the definition of "wyrd." Time and again, the translator is baffled by the opacity of the poem. The work of the translator is as much to understand this extraliterary frame, the mythos of the tribe and its *signa sacra*, as it is to work through the poem word by word.

The translator must use whatever means are available to him to penetrate the context of the poem. He must steep himself in whatever has an Anglo-Saxon, or even northern-medieval, smell to it. During much of the time I worked on this translation, I was living in Reykjavík, Iceland, not far from the National Museum. Often I would stroll through the galleries devoted to artifacts of the *fornöld* and study with quiet attention the objects gathered in one of the glass cases. There were displayed the contents of an ancient burial field. Over the recumbent skeleton of a woman, arranged as she was found, in the posture of sleep, hung a tenth-century sword of non-Icelandic manufacture. The blade was a jagged tusk of rust-corroded iron, but the thread wound about its grip was silver. On its openwork bronze chape traces of the original gilding remained. This sword proved a talisman to my imagination, a materia from deposits perhaps contemporaneous with my poem. It put me in touch with Memory, permitted me to comtemplate the *lāf,* the heirlooms, of a civilization kindred to my poet's.

Of course, attentive study of the Sutton Hoo finds bears even more closely on the translator's work. It almost seems as if the poet gazed upon these objects as he composed his lines. Herbert Maryon, who pieced the vizored helmet together, imagined it "in its original condition as an object of burnished silvery metal, set in a trellis-work of gold, surmounted by a crest of massive silver, and embellished with gilded ornaments, garnets, and niello."[30] Simply as an Anglo-Saxon symbol of power and inheritance, it provides the translator with a tangible image of the magnificent treasure that Hrothgar granted Beowulf and of the luminous things heaped on Scyld's vessel and the dead king's pyre. Beyond providing the translator's imagination with the sensuous forms that he needs to give body and reality to the translated images, it helps him interpret certain difficult words in the poem's helmet passages, for example, "wala" (1031) and "swīn-līcum" (1453).

But even objects like the great gold buckle or the purse flap, which have no analogues in the poem, are of immense importance to the translator. The image of the hawk seizing the duck done in cloisonné with inlay of garnet and mosaic glass; the serpentine interlace of the buckle enhanced by the black outline of the niello—these reveal their makers' "searucræft." Even for the veteran student of Old English they may provide a more palpable touchstone of the Anglo-Saxon's artistic genius than the poem itself.

Finally, the very condition of the find—the sword blade rusted inextricably to its sheath, the stag image broken from the standard, the helmet pieced together from corroded shards by dint of an antiquarian's zeal, and all these luminous heirlooms wasting in the sandy loam—suggests the poet's sense of the corruptible magnificence of earthly treasure, as realized in the "Lay of the Last Survivor" and in the passage in which Wiglaf surveys the dragon hoard and sees "cups standing, / chalices of vanished tribes, their ornaments eaten away, / and none to polish them" (2760b–62a).

Such scholarship as H. R. Ellis Davidson's *The Sword in Anglo-Saxon England* is likewise indispensable—there the translator finds detailed the technology of sword manufacture and a plausible intepretation of various puzzling compounds that refer to swords.[31]

Attempting to ascertain the meaning of a color word like "fealwe" or an abstract concept like "wyrd," the translator comes up against his distance from the poet's mind. He begins to deliberate in terms of Whorfian thought worlds and undescribed cryptotypes. If the Anglo-Saxon mapped his colors differently from the way we do, why not the entire cosmos? If this is so, what kinship is there among cognates? The translator may well begin to question his basis for translating at all: perhaps, he ponders, the authentic translation of *Beowulf* would prove incomprehensible to a modern.

At the very least, the translator fears "overenglishing" the text. He worries that he has maintained "the accidental state of his own language instead of letting it be violently moved"[32] by the Old English. He gazes with admiration at Chickering's dual-language translation that concentrates on reproducing "the poetic ordering of parts, sentence by sentence" and in which "blind references and parataxis" are used to "give some inkling of the craggy sentence structure of the original."[33] There is that vital strangeness, even awkwardness, which Pannwitz considers the hallmark of faithful translation. To paraphrase Pannwitz, Chickering's is an Old English-Modern English rather than a modernized Old English.

It must be pointed out that Chickering's translation faces the original Old English text. It takes its freedom of structure and form from the fact it is meant to be an interlinear, leaning against the old text. As a consequence, Chickering has not had to wrestle overmuch with Steiner's third hermeneutic motion—that of incorporating the meaning and form into Modern English. He cranes his attention more keenly toward the old language, attempting to preserve its syntax and its strangeness.

The translator who intends to bring out his work without the original facing it must contend with the syntax and the sound of his own language, as well as with the structure of Old English. Indeed, his muse might, appropriately, be Janus, the Roman god of doors and beginnings, who was represented with two faces that looked in opposite directions. Ideally, the translator stands at the threshold of both languages, his vigilance equal in both directions.

The translator cannot do this as a god, knowing precisely what came before and what follows after, the absolute meaning of the original (known more wholly than the Saxon poet could have known it) and the total embodiment of that unrealized meaning in Modern English. His apprehension of the original, as has been noted, is confounded at every turn by his ignorance of the language and the culture. And even if he had such clairvoyance, there would face him what faces every writer, his own intractable language.

Yet at times it may happen that the text becomes transparent to the translator, and he is able to steal into the language and steal away with some of its poetic gold and somehow manage to hoard it up in his own language. It happens sometimes—as when Robert Fitzgerald translates the opening lines of *The Odyssey,* or Kevin Crossley-Holland encounters the Old English riddle of the swan—

"Silent is my dress when I step across the earth, / reside in my house, or ruffle the waters."[34] Such moments of transparence imply an affinity between the translator and his text; the translator feels he was meant to translate this poem. The full meaning of "calling" becomes apparent. Belitt speaks of those passages "we can't wait to get to because there is an exhilarating affinity or symbiosis between what comes to us happily and what the text requires of us."[35]

My own affinity to the poem seems to lie in that quality which moved Tolkien to consider the poem "a solemn funeral-ale with the taste of death."[36] Heorot is erected and foredoomed by fire in almost the same breath; Beowulf gazes on Freawaru, who is promised to Ingeld, and foresees slaughter; at the death of Beowulf, the messenger who relays the terrible news foretells the destruction of the tribe. The poet was steeped in a sense of the mortality of things.

The elegiac theme, of course, is nothing unusual in English poetry or, for that matter, in the poetry of all tongues. It is present in *Gilgamesh, The Odyssey,* and the songs of the Aztecs; it is one of the continuities of English verse. When Hrothgar counsels the victorious Beowulf (1700–1784) or when the old man in Beowulf's tale laments his dead son (2444–62), the translator can be confident he comprehends the substance of the verses. As he or she is human, the burden is familiar.

But in *Beowulf* this theme seems almost obsessively developed. According to the poet's vision, all human structures are brittle; time, fire, and man's violent instincts will quickly bring them down. Our own age, poised on the brink of nuclear holocaust, shares much with the poet's elegiac vision. It may indeed seem forced to compare the destruction of a single sixth-century northern tribe with that of our present world civilization, but for the eye of the imagination the essential form is what matters. For the *Beowulf* poet the destruction of the Geats was a metaphor for the frailty of all human things; for us it is the Bomb. At least, this is how I explain my own deep susceptibility to the poem's elegiac vision.

Not everything can be translated now: an age, as well as an individual translator, may lack the sympathy and the insight to read the original with proper understanding. But given this deep-rooted commonalty between the *Beowulf* poet's sense of the fragility of the human condition and our own similar angst, the time may have arrived when the translator of *Beowulf* can collaborate at the level of his own mortality with the old poet.

2
Choosing the Form

> One thing seems clear: to translate a poem whole is to compose another poem. A whole translation will be faithful to the *matter*, and it will "approximate the form," of the original.
> —Jackson Mathews

Beowulf is a poem, "a machine made of words," as William Carlos Williams would say. To provide an approximation of the density of its structure, the careful patterning of its sound and syntax—its "poemness"—the translator must use a verse form to "approximate the form" of the original. It can, of course, be argued that prose permits greater fidelity to the thought and expression of the original—the prose translator need not skew meaning and alter image to satisfy an abstract pattern of rhythm or meter. And certainly for the purpose of supplying the student of Old English with an interlinear, an aid to study, the prose version may be the more useful. My bias is otherwise: to ignore the rhythm and the aural patterning of the verses is to betray *Beowulf*'s artistry.

E. T. Donaldson foregrounds a single stylistic technique in his prose translation: "the extraordinary richness of rhetorical elaboration alternating with—often combined with—the barest simplicity of statement."[1] Donaldson's justification for his literal version is, finally, that it should be used as a study aid, a pony: "Rather than try to create a new and lesser poem for the reader, it seems better to offer him in prose the literal materials from which he can re-create the poem."[2] It is rather startling to think that one could simply add aesthetic niceties to the "literal materials" and so "re-create the poem" rather like reconstituting whole milk from a dehydrated mix. This thrusts the completion of the third hermeneutic motion into the reader's hands. It is as if the translator has no heart for the task.

David Wright, another translator who used prose, wishes to foreground the narrative structure of the poem. Since "one of the poetic virtues of a primary epic is to be found in its construction, plot and narrative interest,"[3] he concentrates on these qualities, aiming "not to distract the reader's attention from the story that is presented by the poet of *Beowulf* by attempting to recreate his allusive use of language."[4] This would indeed corroborate Frost's definition of poetry as the stuff that is lost in translation. The translator sacrifices the poem to the story and to his all-too-vivid awareness "that he is a writer of contemporary English prose competing with other writers of contemporary English prose for the attention of his readers."[5] And so his translation becomes a casualty of his overzealous fidelity to his imagined reader and of his Malthusian literary vision.

A brief look at the poem itself shows immediately what is lost in a prose translation:

> Ða cōm of mōre   under misthleoþum
> Grendel gongan,   Godes yrre bær;
> mynte se mānscaða   manna cynnes
> sumne besyrwan   in sele þām hēan.
>
> (710–13)

The distinctive features of the Old English verse line are readily visible: the balanced, two-beat half-lines linked across the caesura by alliteration; the predilection for a falling rhythm; and the overall rhythmic variety within this basic paradigm. The sense, the emphasis, is generated by the hammer blows of the stresses: "GRENdel GONgan,   GODes yrre BÆR." The repeated falling rhythm of the first half-line, coupled with the alliterating "G" suggests the monster's relentless footfall; yet the power is countered, as it were, across the caesura by the wrath of God, with the final stress placed on "bær" where it lingers on this, the final syllable of the verse. It cannot profit Grendel that the stress lies so heavily there and the line is end-stopped, intensifying that stress. The rhythm can be imagined as setting up a tension between Grendel's might and God's wrath, and even as foreshadowing Grendel's fall. Rhythm in this passage is not an ornament that can be dispensed with. It generates meaning; it works along the reader's pulse to intensify the experience of Grendel's implacable movement.

Donaldson's prose reads: "Then from the moor under the mist-hills Grendel came walking, wearing God's anger. The foul ravager thought to catch some one of mankind there in the high hall."[6] The rhythmic emphases are gone and with them Grendel's thunderous footfall and the juxtaposition of Grendel's and God's power. "The foul ravager thought" lacks the energetic drive which incarnates Grendel's active will toward mischief in the half-line, "mynte se mānscaða." A poem in verse demands a verse translation. Having determined this, however, the translator is still faced with the difficult task of choosing the verse form.

The verse translators of *Beowulf* have tried as many meters as their ingenuity and inventiveness have provided. It is humbling to know they all sought to preserve the poetry; for the efforts of the early translators such as Wackerbarth and Lumsden now seem quaint and, not infrequently, comic in their choice of diction and rhythm. In 1849, Wackerbarth published the first complete translation of the poem, written in ballad measure, which Edwin Morgan considers "so quaintly and so wildly unlike the high seriousness of the original that it is almost attractive, like a double parody, first of *Beowulf* and then of the ballad."[7] A few of Wackerbarth's lines will bear out Morgan's judgment:

> —And ill I ween, though prov'd thy Might
> In onslaught dire and deadly Fight,
> 'Twill go with thee, if thou this Night
> Dar'st wait for Grendel bold.[8]

Lumsden (1881), Leonard (1923), and Strong (1925) used various sorts of rhyming couplets. Leonard's "Niebulungen couplets" have the distinction of being praised by Frederick Klaeber and ridiculed by both Morgan and Burton Raffel.[9] Leonard's rhythmic paradigm is immediately apparent in his opening lines: "What ho! We've heard the glory of   Spear-Danes, clansmen-kings / Their deeds of olden story,—   how fought the aethelings."[10] He has modeled his entire translation on the rhythm of "Sing a Song of Six Pence"![11]

Both Conybeare, in his specimen extracts of 1826, and Mary Waterhouse, in her 1949 translation, used blank verse as their medium. Waterhouse explains her choice of form:

> The metre, no less than the words of *Beowulf*, requires translation for the modern ear. The Old English verse form is too unfamiliar to be acceptable to those who are not students. . . . These considerations led to the choice of blank verse as the medium, taking it as the modern heroic line and therefore the equivalent of the older one.[12]

Both Morgan and Francis Gummere, however, deem blank verse inappropriate. Gummere considers Conybeare's blank verse too smooth:

It is idle to answer that the translation reads well. It reads better than the original, for that matter. It reads too well. One travels better in a Pullman car than in a stage-coach; but suppose our object is to revive the sensations of the old-fashioned journey?[13]

Further, Gummere claims that "the language of blank verse, more than of any other kind, is what Arnold calls 'a literary and intellectualized language.'"[14] The form is steeped in associations with Marlowe, Shakespeare, and Milton; it has become the language of the "grand epic," which is an "absolutely different creation from the primitive epic—Homer, *Beowulf*."[15] Gummere's is a sensitive observation. The associations of blank verse are altogether inappropriate for *Beowulf;* the form is a violation of the old poem, an anachronism.

Interestingly, Morgan judges that the adoption of blank verse archaizes rather than modernizes *Beowulf*. It is important to note that he is writing seventy years later than Gummere. By his time—the early 1950s—he contends that the "adoption of blank verse in translation has the effect of a metrical archaizing, and is merely another barrier between reader and original."[16] There is no "modern heroic line" because "there is no tradition of modern heroic poetry; and blank verse is no longer a living medium for extended writing."[17]

This must be all the more true for the translator working in the late 1980s. Although the past decade has seen a resurgence of interest in formal metrical patterns by younger poets,[18] most contemporary poets do not use traditional metrical forms. The younger American poets write a free verse attentive to contemporary American speech rhythms. Translators since the fifties have followed suit: they have seen fit to "free the verse" of even the formal poets they translate. Robert Bly used no rhymes in his translations of *The Sonnets to Orpheus;* Galway Kinnell translated Villon using his hardboiled free-verse line. Robert Lowell, in his Introduction to his 1961 *Imitations*, writes deprecatingly of "strict metrical translators", even while he allows the sprawling sameness of the "now fashionable translations into free or irregular verse."[19]

Because of these tendencies any highly structured form is going to appear somewhat dated, if not antiquated, to an American audience. Certainly this applies to blank verse; perhaps Edwin Muir was the last poet to use the form with a natural proficiency, and Muir, for all his modern sensibility, had deep ties to the formal oral traditions of his native Orkney. Before Muir, Browning, Tennyson, and Wordsworth made blank verse the medium for the dramatic monologue in the nineteenth century. While a case might be made for translating the dialogues of *Beowulf* into blank verse, to cast the entire poem in this form would be an error in poetic tact.

Granted that the use of blank verse for *Beowulf* is a species of mistranslation, brave effects should still be possible in a form that Milton and Shakespeare exalted. Let us see how Waterhouse handles the form:

> Then from the moor beneath the misty hills
> Grendel striding came, God's curse he bore;
> The miscreant intended to ensnare
> Many a man within the lofty hall.
> Beneath the clouds he went to where he knew
> Full well the palace stood, men's treasure hall,
> Bright with its golden plating. Nor was that
> The first time he had sought out Hrothgar's home;
> Yet never he in life before or since
> Came upon thanes in hall with harder fortune.[20]

There are some interesting lines here. Waterhouse varies the rhythm, and substitutes a trochee for an iamb, now and again, as in "Grendel striding came, God's curse he bore." Yet even here the inverted foot has dragged along with it an inverted syntax that grates against our intuitions of English sentence form. And Waterhouse often pads her rhythm with those dull little words—prepositions, articles, and adjectives—that create a slack rhythm: "Beneath the clouds he went to where he knew / Full well the palace stood, men's treasure hall." A more accomplished practitioner of blank verse could no doubt achieve more vigorous rhythms and so make the form appear more appropriate. As it is, the full potential of blank verse remains unrealized.

More recently, Stanley Greenfield used "a nine-syllable line for regular Old English verse, and an eleven-syllable for hypermetric lines."[21] Greenfield explains:

This number of syllables seems a natural equivalent for the Anglo-Saxon poetic line: it allows for the flexibility of modern verse—the caesura can be placed anywhere from after the first to after the eighth syllable—and yet provides a slight restraint that is suggestive of the fixity of the Old English verse form without simulating the metrical scheme.[22]

This seems too arbitrary a choice since one of the salient features of the Old English verse line is its variable length, even as it holds to its four-stress pattern. While narrating travel or movement, the lines may become short and brisk:

>   þæt ðā līðende   land gesāwon,
>   brimclifu blīcan,   beorgas stēape,
>   sīde sænæssas;   Þā wæs sund liden,
>   eoletes æt ende. . . .
>
>   (221–24a)

Or the line can lengthen for the sake of ceremony and move in a slow cadence, as when Hrothgar remembers the dominion that once was his:

>   Swā ic Hring-Dena   hund missēra
>   wēold under wolcnum   ond hig wigge belēac
>   manigum mǣgþa   geond þysne middangeard,
>   æscum ond ecgum,   þæt ic mē ǣnigne
>   under swegles begong   gesacan ne tealde.
>
>   (1769–73)

To capture this quality, Morgan asks that the translated "line must be able to contract to terseness and expand to splendour."[23] Granted, Greenfield's syllabics allow for the flexibility of modern verse, but they permit him neither the freedom nor the restraint of the Old English verse line.

In keeping with the modernist aesthetic of translation, Greenfield's principles require that the translator's metrical system "be equivalent to but not the same as, the Old English alliterative verse."[24] Further, it should "have a fixity that suggests, but does not ape, the restraint of the four-stress heavily caesuraed Anglo-Saxon line."[25]

To bolster his argument, Greenfield cites Morgan's arguments regarding metrical equivalency, yet Morgan has argued more persuasively than anyone that the four-beat line used by Eliot, Auden, and Eberhart provides the translator with a viable meter ready to hand. Indeed, Eberhart's elegiac and martial lament, "Brotherhood of Men," has a strong Anglo-Saxon flavor, both in its vision and rhythm:

>   And never in after years those left to live
>   Would treat with truth those savage times,
>   And sometimes wish that they had died
>   As did those many crying in their arms.[26]

It might be argued that some of the most distinguished verse of this century has been written in strong stress meter. Yeats began his career by writing in triple meter, in imitation of Swinburne, but he grew dissatisfied with "those energetic rhythms, as of a man running."[27] By mid-career, he was frequently using strong stress meter, as in "Easter 1916," which is written in three-stress lines. Yeats's penultimate play, *Purgatory,* exhibits a norm of four stresses per verse line. Like the old English verse line, his line is extremely variable in length. Interestingly, Harvey Gross judges that Yeats's use of this form represents his solution to the problem of discovering "a poetic medium close to contemporary speech, unrelated to Shakespeare's blank verse, yet capable of rhythmic emphasis at moments of dramatic intensity."[28]

The later Eliot, like the later Yeats, also explored the strong stress line. While *The Four Quartets* represents a *tour de force* in rhythmic composition, the four-stress line provides its normative rhythm:

> Dry the pool, dry concrete, brown edged,
> And the pool was filled with water out of sunlight,
> And the lotos rose, quietly, quietly,
> The surface glittered out of heart of light.[29]

Add to this distinguished list Ezra Pound, W. H. Auden, Dylan Thomas, Theodore Roethke, and Basil Bunting, and the contemporary translator of *Beowulf* need make no apologies for choosing a four-stress line. As both A. J. Bliss and Marjorie Daunt have pointed out, strong stress rhythm is still native to contemporary English speech, despite the numerous sound changes since Anglo-Saxon times.[30] Daunt even goes so far as to analyze, according to Eduard Siever's system, a 1939 shoe advertisement in the *Evening News*. She concludes that the rhythm found in Old English verse "has survived for centuries and is still largely the mould in which we cast our speech, unless a Latinate rhythm is superimposed by a special education, and even then the native swing often emerges."[31] Roethke corroborates this by noting that, "while our genius in the language may be essentially iambic, particularly in the formal lyric, much of memorable or passionate speech is strongly stressed, irregular, even 'sprung,' if you will."[32] Roethke may have taken counsel here from his old master, Yeats. In any event, their poetic practices demonstrate that strong stress rhythm is allied to modern colloquial speech and passionate utterance and is still a vital aspect of our tongue.

Thus to choose the four-stress line is not a question of servilely aping the Old English line, as Greenfield suggests; rather, the line is modern, as well as ancient, and reveals one of the striking continuities of English verse and the English language.

Not surprisingly, many translators of *Beowulf* have used this form—Charles Kennedy, Edwin Morgan, Michael Alexander, and Kevin Crossley-Holland. Even before Yeats and Eliot recovered the line for general poetic use, Gummere and Scott Moncrieff composed their translations in strong stress rhythms.

Perhaps the greatest danger faced by the translator who elects to imitate the old form lies in his use of alliteration. Wyld counsels the translator to use alliteration sparingly, if at all;[33] the modern reader does not share the Saxon's pleasure in frequent alliteration. He, like Chaucer's parson, scorns the *rum, ram, ruf* as archaic. This is sensible advice, as, I believe, this passage from Michael Alexander's highly alliterative translation bears witness:

> This gold was to be on the neck of the grandson of Swerting
> on the last of his harryings, Higelac the Geat,
> as he stood before the standard astride his plunder,
> defending his war-haul: Weird struck him down;
> in his superb pride he provoked disaster
> in the Frisian feud. This fabled collar
> the great war-king wore when he crossed
> the foaming waters; he fell beneath his shield.
> The king's person passed into Frankish hands.[34]

Alexander has tried faithfully to suggest the alliteration of the Old English line; unfortunately, he has ignored the tastes of his contemporary audience. To us, the lines sound tricked up. Morgan uses more discretion; he alliterates, but not so frequently:

> The next possessor of that ring-jewel
> Was Hygelac of the Geats, Swerting's grandson,
> From the time when his banner guarded the treasure,
> Defended the war-booty; he was seized by fate
> When for glory's sake he courted misery
> In Frisian's enmity. Those jewels he took,
> The powerful prince, those rare stones over
> The brimming waves; and by his shield he fell.[35]

Morgan's lines are also superior to Alexander's because the rhythms and phrasing are closer to natural speech patterns. Compare Morgan's lines 1202–3 to Alexander's "This gold was to be on the neck of the grandson of Swerting." This is neither Old

English nor Modern. Alexander's verse is wrenched into unnatural patterns by what may be called alliteration exigency.

Daunt and Bliss have both argued that the rhythms of *Beowulf* are the rhythms of spoken Old English.[36] Admittedly, their conclusions are speculative, and Thomas Cable has challenged them in a convincing manner.[37] Yet the bias of the translator's age is for a poetry that does not distance itself overmuch from the vernacular, either in rhythm or diction, and so he must find Daunt's and Bliss's conclusions convenient, even while he concedes that they may be mistaken. In the next chapter, I will take a more conservative, and apparently inconsistent, position regarding diction. I do this because of the practical judgment that artificial rhythms, given the modern bias, will estrange the translator's potential audience in a way formal diction will not.

In any event, if the poets of this century have any common ground, it is on the need to bring verse closer to the spoken language. Yeats, Eliot, Williams, and Frost, for all their differences, labored toward this common end. (Yeats, as I noted, "rediscovered" strong stress meter to achieve this.) The last two generations of poets writing in English have gone even further in this direction.

For this reason, the translator should select from the rhythms of contemporary spoken English, just as the *Beowulf* poet may have selected from the rhythms of spoken Old English. Here J. R. R. Tolkien, as elsewhere, has much to teach the translator. In "The Homecoming of Beorhtnoth Beorhthelm's Son" he writes in a meter strongly imitative of the Old English system:

> They've had their fill of hewing and fighting,
> and picked their plunder: the place is bare.
> They're in Ipswich now with the ale running,
> or lying off London in their long vessels,
> while they drink to Thor and drown the sorrow
> of hell's children. These are hungry folk
> and masterless men, miserable skulkers.[38]

These lines suggest that Tolkien would agree with Daunt that "Old English verse is really conditioned prose, i.e., the spoken language specially arranged with alliteration, but arranged in a way that does no violence to the spoken words."[39] The rhythm of Tolkien's lines is that of spoken Modern English and yet they are easily analyzable according to Siever's system. The caesura has been kept, but partly concealed. The incidence of alliteration is even greater than that found in Alexander's lines. Yet, the poet has done no violence to the patterns of spoken words to achieve this alliteration: the rhythm and syntax are quite natural. Instead, the alliteration dignifies the lines, as it must have in the Old English verses.

3
Diction

> If you wish to translate, not rewrite *Beowulf,* your language must be literary and traditional: not because it is now a long while since the poem was made, or because it speaks of things that have since become ancient: but because the diction of *Beowulf* was poetical, archaic, artificial (if you will), in the day that the poem was made.
> —J. R. R. Tolkien

1

The translator in 1989 faces *Beowulf* over an abyss that might well silence him. It is not merely that his readings of hundreds of words must remain provisional, or that the triumph of positivism has banished Grendel and the dragon to that realm of suppressed desires we all are said to carry within us, or that the comitatus, which operates in *Beowulf* as pervasively as the law of gravity, is a social form as alien to us as a Kwakiutl potlatch. While any of the above might well discourage the translator from ever committing his pen to the page, even more vexing is the problem of diction raised by Tolkien's counsel.

To its Anglo-Saxon audience, the diction of *Beowulf* immediately established that the poet's theme was to be heroic, some legend drawn from its shared memory, some record of beginnings, or else a sacred Christian story. If not exactly the language of the gods, the diction of *Beowulf* represents the higher level of the Anglo-Saxon lexicon, reserved for speech of "high sentence" and noble purpose. It was retrospective in a way we cannot fathom—the very ancientness of the words providing a sort of objective correlative of memory. Eighteenth-century poetic language such as "watery shore" or "fleecy care" only faintly resembles what was in Anglo-Saxon times a true language of poetry—a language that at times seemed "dark" to its original audience and even, perhaps, to the poets who inherited the lexicon. Uncertainty of meaning was not eschewed for the recollection, and honoring, of ancient things. One thinks of the incantatory power the Latin mass exercised over the Catholic laity until recently. The Anglo-Saxon poet often stresses what is not, or cannot, be known, and the *Beowulf* poet is no exception (cf. 50b–52; 1366b–67b).

This is, of course, foreign to our contemporary habits of speech and to our poetry. Both Henry Wyld and Tolkien encourage the translator of *Beowulf* to use a traditional poetic language,[1] yet the modernist revolution has swept such language away. There is no poetic diction anymore except among the writers of greeting card verse.

Such was not always the case, even in fairly recent times. Geoffrey Leech notes that "in the period 1600–1900 there vaguely existed what could be called a 'standard archaic usage' for English poetry, not based on the style of any one writer."[2] In the mid-eighteenth century this tendency for poets to use an inherited poetic diction became fixed briefly into an idea of decorum. To use such language implied that the poet was conversant with the norms of good taste; poetic diction linked a new work to the body of past poetry, investing it with seriousness and solemnity. Thomas Gray could write to a friend in 1742, "The language of the age is never the language of poetry."[3]

This literary tradition still informed the judgments of Wyld and Tolkien concerning poetic diction and the translation of *Beowulf*. Yet the converse of Gray's statement is true today: the whole of the English language in its current form has been made available to the poet.[4] Other significant changes as well have altered the poet's relationship to his language. F. W. Bateson notes:

> The problem of diction has been simplified for the modern poet by the fact that we are much less sensitive to the connotations of words than our fathers and grandfathers were. A word is taken more at its face-value nowadays. It is not so liable to explode if brought into contact with words of which the associations are different. But the language, if less explosive, is also less emphatic than it was, and it is this lack of emphasis, this hesitancy, that is the characteristic defect of contemporary poetry. A modern poet wears an air of self-conscious casuality. He seems to be thinking aloud; his poems have the abruptness and untidiness of thought in the raw.[5]

If this is an accurate assessment, the consequences bear profoundly on the problem of the choice of diction facing the contemporary translator. Whereas the Anglo-Saxon poet relied on what might be called the chiaroscuro effects—the shadowy connotations—of his words,[6] the rage now is for precision and absolute clarity of image. Williams's revolutionary statement of 1920 has become dogma in our writing workshops:

> When a man makes a poem, makes it, mind you, he takes words as he finds them interrelated about him and composes them—without distortion which would mar their exact significances—into an intense expression of his perceptions and his ardors that they may constitute a revelation of the speech that he uses.[7]

Williams's entire oeuvre is an exercise in "exact significance"— he tried to ferret out and use a word's precise denotation. Modern poetry, in America and Britain at least, has followed Williams in this tendency. Denotative language has been foregrounded. The contemporary poet does not use words as diffuse echoes of the sacred hoard of previous generations of work, but as the hard definite levers that, when touched, yield precise meanings.

The two ages could not be more distinct in their attitudes toward the language of poetry. In one, the use of poetic diction is an absolute requirement; in the other, anathema; in one, the traditional register is lofty and aristocratic, appropriate for the discourse of kings and angels; in the other, the accepted usage is the democratic middle voice, appropriate for a person speaking to others (preferably in informal circumstances); in one, the word is hieratic, the very signum of Memory, honored for its darkness as well as for its light; in the other, the word is a linguistic phenomenon, the simian's tool for signifying reality, distrusted because of its unavoidable imprecision.

As the Janus of these opposing visions of the word, these two distinct thought worlds, the translator owes his allegiance to both. Is there, however, any conceivable middle way? Or must the translator's fidelity to one age be the measure of his betrayal of the other?

The translator cannot, as Wyld and Tolkien counsel, use the worn-out periphrases that were dead before his parents were born, much less rescue the archaic words of the poem itself, as William Morris tried to do. The danger is self-evident in this translation by James Garnett published in 1895:

> He taketh forced pledge, he spareth no one
> Of the Dane's people, but he joy beareth,
> Killeth and eateth, nor weeneth of contest
> With the Spear-Danes.[8]

This is not what Walter Benjamin had in mind when he wrote of the need for the translated poem to possess a vital strangeness. All of the translations written before 1940 suffer from a superfluity of archaic diction. Even the tactful Charles Kennedy, whose translation of *Beowulf* appeared in 1940, does not avoid archaism:

> Then out spoke Unferth, Ecglaf's son,
> Who sat at the feet of the Scylding lord,
> Picking a quarrel—for Beowulf's quest,
> His bold sea-voyaging, irked him sore.[9]
>
> (499–502)

Here the archaism "irked him sore" is accompanied, as it habitually is in such translations, by the arrangement of syntactic elements in an irregular order, hyperbaton, a feature common to premodernist poetry.

With regard to archaism, Morgan takes a hard, pragmatic line, and counsels: "There is no use being faithful to the poetic archaisms of the original if the result cannot be couched in terms acceptable to one's poetic co-readers and co-writers. If it is a case of losing an archaism or losing the poetry, the archaism must go."[10]

Yet Morgan states the choice too extremely. To suppress the archaism does not necessarily mean that the translator must choose the absolutely contemporary. While he lacks the gold of an inherited poetic diction, the translator can still select from the spoken language words of nobler register and higher tone. The more tradition-conscious modern poets—Yeats, Eliot, and Stevens—achieved such a language. The poetry of Yeats after 1920 with its spare, dignified language, its strong stress rhythms, and its remembrance of heroic things, might well serve the translator as a touchstone:

> Two heavy trestles, and a board,
> Where Sato's gift, a changeless sword,
> By pen and paper lies . . .
> A bit of embroidered dress
> Covers its wooden sheath.
> Chaucer had not drawn breath
> When it was forged. In Sato's house
> Curved like new moon, moon-luminous
> It lay five hundred years.[11]

Here is a Janus-faced language, both modern and ancient, dignified, yet bearing the accents of the speaking human voice. The colloquial and the formal mingle to great effect: the informal and off-handed "A bit of embroidered dress" is followed by the stately and ceremonial "Chaucer had not drawn breath / When it was forged." The late Yeats has what may be called, if somewhat paradoxically, a plain and stately style. By dint of passion and an extraordinary ear for the rhythms of spoken English, Yeats made a retrospective and conservative diction seem contemporary.

In fact, if one ignores his plea for the use of traditional poetic diction, Tolkien prescribes just such a formal register in his preface to Clark's translation:

> But, whether you regret it or not, you will misrepresent the first and most salient characteristic of the style and flavour of the author, if in translating *Beowulf*, you deliberately eschew the traditional literary and poetic diction which we now possess in favour of the current and trivial. . . . The things we are here dealing with are serious, moving, and full of "high sentence"—if we have the patience and solidity to endure them for awhile. We are being at once wisely aware of our own frivolity and just to the solemn temper of the original, if we avoid *hitting* and *whacking* and prefer "striking" and "smiting"; *talk* and *chat* and prefer "speech" and "discourse".[12]

Tolkien's own practice, as was seen in "The Homecoming of Beorhtnoth Beorhthelm's Son," involves a selection from the rhythms of spoken Modern English. These rhythms carry on their backs a retrospective diction that, like Yeats's, seems almost contemporary:

> day follows day, and the dust gathers,
> his tomb crumbles, as time gnaws it,
> and his kith and kindred out of ken dwindle.
> So men flicker and in the mirk go out.
> The world withers and the wind rises;
> the candles are quenched. Cold falls the night.[13]

The informed poet, like the translator, knows that certain of our most modern-sounding words are inherited from the Anglo-Saxons; such words—day, dust, flicker, and quenched—though ancient, are the enduring currency of our speech.

Even Edwin Morgan, who is a vigorous opponent of archaism, uses a diction that does not sound contemporary:

> Hrothgar spoke, protector of the Scyldings:
> "In memory of deeds done, in the service of honour
> You have come to visit us, Beowulf my friend.

> Your father instigated the greatest of feuds;
> Heatholaf he killed with his own hands
> Among the Wylfings; and the Weder-folk
> Didn't dare hold him for fear of invasion.[14]
>
> (456–62)

Morgan's translation of Hrothgar's speech opens with two ceremonial prepositional phrases, delaying the presentation of the subject and characterizing Beowulf's fidelity, even before he is mentioned. Line 459 has a more modern ring to it with the Latinate "instigated" (the OED records its first use in 1542, but it was not used as it is in the above passage, with the meaning "to bring about incitement or persuasion," until 1852).[15] The hyperbaton of "Heatholaf he killed" again suggests older patterns of syntax. By such means, the translator glances toward both the past and the present. Throughout, Morgan achieves an effective blend of the ancient and the modern. His tact in the matter, however, is not absolutely sure; he is capable of eccentric choices and at times exhibits a latinate, Miltonic tendency:

> He aimed to divide, before day came,
> Monstrous in frightfulness, life from limb
> In every man of them, now that he had hope
> Of ravening to gluttonousness. But the fate was finished
> That could keep him after that night carnivorous
> On human kind.[16]
>
> (731–36)

The enterprise of translation depends on tact—on finding the right register, the clairvoyant mix of ancient and modern, the *mot juste*. The theorist can offer no absolute prescriptions, but he can suggest reasonable biases. I would venture that if a successful translation of *Beowulf* is ever written, it will have a diction that is modern and yet possessed of that patina which Yeats's diction exhibits. This aged modernness was not for Yeats an easy acquisition but I suspect it came partly from an ear attentive to the rhythms of the English he heard spoken in Dublin in 1920, as well as from a memory steeped in the entire tradition of English poetry from Chaucer forward. The translator needs such an exquisite ear and such a grasp of the tradition.

Still, even a gifted translator can play the game too safely. Steering along this middle path, the translator is more likely to achieve mediocrity than excellence. Some authority beyond the scope of common sense, an eros directed at the life of the translator's language as well as at the original poem, may be the real instrument of the translator's genius. I have, for instance, viewed archaisms with disdain if not repugnance. Yet some of the greatest efforts of translation have been made by writers seeking to weld two languages together through extreme effects of diction and syntax. In his translations of Pindar and Sophocles, Hölderlin sought "to wrench meaning out of its Greek carapace by force of word-for-word transposition."[17] Using Swabian forms and Old High German, Hölderlin worked backwards toward the source of Germanic speech and "to the primal energies of human discourse."[18] Similarly, Rudolph Borchardt translated Dante into a weird construct of "bits of High, Low, and Middle High German"[19] in an attempt to reinfuse modern German with some of the vitality and potentiality he thought it had lost because of Luther. He wanted, in fact, to rewrite or revise the German tongue.

The English translator of *Beowulf* finds himself in a position where, had he such ambitions and the genius to realize them, he might make some contribution to the renewal of his language. Such a renewal would most likely occur at the level of diction. I am not speaking of the reintroduction into Modern English of words that have lain fallow in the *Beowulf* manuscript for a thousand years. Indeed, I have used the word "aetheling" now and again, but only with great reluctance, because none of its modern equivalents—nobleman or prince or knight—carries the sense of a man of royal blood and bearing whose every deed exudes nobility. I have done this hoping the reader, while first raising an eyebrow at the curious word, will learn its meaning from the context and come to accept it, perhaps even to appreciate its aptness.

What I wish to suggest, rather, is that our age is amnesic, and our use of words suggests this amnesia. The arts, of course, reflect this condition. When Williams made his now-famous assertion— "No ideas but in things"—and sought a highly denotative language, he was, in effect, attempting to expunge the memory of tradition and the murkiness of connotations, which he considered a hindrance to clear perception and to an accurate apprehension of the Terra Nova, the American place. That act of erasure was salutary in 1920; it is no longer. The word everywhere is being stripped of meaning, becoming a mere ghostly counter of a statistical and uncertain reality: stripped of its connotation and its etymology, it becomes the thin, brittle thing that transmits the evening news, or the bureaucrat's in-house study on limited nuclear options (LNOS), or the amber script on the screens of our word-processors. Divorced from its past, the word withers into a husk that may be used without thought for the most barbarous purposes. It may be this general ghostliness of the word that is responsible for that "air of casuality" that Bateson writes of or the strange fact that Donald Davie noted—"the best modern poems often read as if they were good translations from another language."[20] The poet today finds himself in the unenviable position of having to forge his own koine and to establish its significance through his poems.

By turning toward the past and listening intently to the old words, the translator might help renew the substance of his own modern speech and forge links that bind his own words to the hard, interlinked fabric of the Old English.

Beowulf is an utterly mnemonic structure: while scholarly opinion avers it is the work of a writer and not a wandering scop, the poem possesses structural features (formulaic phrases, alliteration, a regular four-stress rhythm) that make it, literally, memorable. The retrospective diction is an aspect of this and so is the imagery—the swords, cups, and plaited metal of a vanished age—as well as the plot with all its memory-laden digressions. The poem can be seen as Memory made palpable. What better medicine for amnesia than a stern dose of Memory?

If the translation of *Beowulf* is genuine, there ought to be some sense, on the reader's part, of rubbing shoulders with something strange and ancient. If the translator chooses his words carefully, they ought to suggest the vanished time and its brilliant equipage. They themselves ought to have the luster of long-buried coins suddenly brought to light. If possible, they ought to have something fey, as well as ancient, about them—like a torch borne solemnly along a windy cliff. So, at least, I have sought in many passages that fugitive prescience of time's sway over all our human moments:

> In his grief he gazes on his son's house,
> the deserted hall, the draughty fire-place
> where the wind is chattering—the horseman sleeps,
> the soldier in his sepulchre; there is no stirring
> of harp or hawk as there was before.
> He turns then to his bed, the one alone
> sings a grief-song for the absent one—
> all too spacious the plains and the dwelling places.
>
> (2455–62)

2

The other large question about diction that faces the translator of *Beowulf* has to do with how he should handle the compounds and kennings. Anyone who has read twenty lines into *Beowulf* knows the poet made exceptional use of the compound and the kenning, what Gavin Bone called the "gripped epithet (the noun holding another noun or adjective in a vice, so that it can't get away but shares its life with the noun, and forms a compound name)."[21] For Arthur Brodeur, compounds are "the richest and most meaningful content words in the poetic vocabulary."[22] Noting that most of these substantive and adjective compounds appear in no other existing texts, Brodeur concludes that the *Beowulf* poet "was the greatest master among all those poets who composed in Anglo-Saxon England, great enough to make the inherited modes serve his ends."[23] The compounds, then, are the very signature of the poet's genius and a constant challenge to the translator's ingenuity.

With Brodeur, I distinguish between two sorts of Old English periphrasis—the kenning and the *kent heiti*. Brodeur restricts "the term kenning to those periphrastic appellations in the base word of which a person or a thing is identified with something which it actually is *not*, except in a very special and artificial sense."[24] That is to say, the kenning "wælrāpa" (water-fetter) refers to ice, but ice is no fetter except in the realm of metaphor. On the other hand, Brodeur uses "the term *kent heiti* for those more direct periphrases which identify the referent with something that it *is* (e.g. 'wave-traverser' for 'ship,' 'heath-stepper' for 'stag,' 'breaker of rings' for 'king')."[25]

The Anglo-Saxon poet delighted in periphrases. While the modern poet relies predominantly on metaphor and simile to reveal unexpected similitudes, the Old English poets used kennings, which are a sort of condensed metaphor with the referent suppressed. "Hronrād" (whale's riding place) is the common example drawn from the poem. To figure out the referent, one might pose a question like "If whales had a riding place, what would it be?" As it is an accessible kenning, one rapidly answers "sea." But one does not disregard the vehicle once one has determined the tenor, unless, of course, the metaphor is dead. Usually, one considers the tenor under a particular aspect—in this case, the ocean is imagined as a region where whales have their riding places. Caroline Brady, for instance, has shown how "hronrād" is probably very different in connotation from "swanrād," another kenning for the sea: "hronrād" refers "to the *expanse* of the ocean—the limitless, trackless, deep sea."[26] "Swanrād" designates an expanse of water "which can be and is crossed with a minimum of difficulty."[27] Her conclusions should not surprise us, given the very different associations the two creatures summon up. To the Saxons, as to us, the whale must have suggested strength, hugeness, and the unknown powers of the sea, while the swan suggested swiftness, smallness, and a delicate beauty.

The kenning always has this riddling quality—indeed, sometimes to such an extent that the modern reader cannot decipher it. Contemporary poets have not given up the ancient game. The kenning is as fully the mark of Dylan Thomas's style as it was of the Old English poet's: he used such kennings as "owl-light" for "moonlight" (?) and "appletowns" for "apple orchards" (with a glance back at the first such orchard). The Northumbrian poet Basil Bunting reclaimed the kenning and the compound for his poetry, although his use of them is not so eccentric and private as Thomas's.

So this continuity enables the modern reader of *Beowulf* to savor an essential texture of the poem. Still, the poet's nominalizing tendency, which seems to go hand in hand with his genius, challenges the translator. Consider lines 321b–28a, in which the poet describes Beowulf's troop in its fearful equipage:

```
                          Gūðbyrne scān
     heard hondlocen,    hringīren scīr
     song in searwum,    þā hīe tō sele furðum
     in hyra gryregeatwum    gangan cwōmon.
     Setton sǣmēþe    sīde scyldas,
     rondas regnhearde    wið þæs recedes weal;
     bugon þā tō bence,—    byrnan hringdon,
     gūðsearo gumena.
```

This is something of a *tour de force;* Brodeur justly lavishes much space on the analysis of its compounds.[28] A fairly literal translation would go like this:

> *War-gear* shone, hard, *linked-by-hand,* bright *iron rings* sang in the harness, when they to the hall in their *terror-gear* first came. They set down, the *sea-weary, broad-shields* against the wall of the building; they sat down at the bench—mail-coats rang, the *war-equipage* of men.

Seven compounds in as many lines. Further, six of the seven compounds occur here and here alone in the extant corpus of Old

English poetry. Thus, we are not dealing with formulaic phrases, inherited variations of "armor" plugged into the poem, according to the exigencies of the verse form. Here the poet is forging an original music by exploiting the nominalizing tendency of his language. Particularly striking, I think, are "hondlocen" and "hringīren"—they give us a powerfully sensuous apprehension of the stout, hand-linked rings of the mail-coat. And the strange, metaphoric "gryregeatwum"—terror-gear—sums up what Hrothgar's thanes must have felt when they saw the unfamiliar, iron-sheathed men approaching. The passage is a synesthetic weld of light, sound, and palpable substance. The mail-coats glittering in the hard sunlight, the bright sounds of the interlinked iron rings, the purposive movements of the armored men—all are expertly registered by the poet. The image is compounded from equal parts of beauty and terror.

Let us see how two translators have handled the compounds in the passage. First, Edwin Morgan:

> War-chains shone,
> Strong-linked, hand-locked, glittering ring-mail
> Gave iron song-of-arms as they first approached
> Marching on to the hall terrible in their battle-trappings.
> Their broad shields they laid, the weary seafarers,
> Hardest of bucklers at the wall of the building,
> And sat at the bench.—The armour rang,
> The war-gear of those men.[29]

Clearly, Morgan favors keeping the compounds—he too has seven, adding two of his own—"strong-linked" and "song-of-arms"—and eliminating two—"sǣmēþe" (sea-weary) and "regnhearde" (wondrous-hard). The savagely compact "gryregeatwum" has been diffused: "terrible in their battle trappings." Yet, the overall effect has been preserved. The compound adjectives "strong-linked" and "hand-locked" admirably serve to suggest the substance and structure of a woven mail-coat; that hard, hand-locked texture of the entire passage has been faithfully translated.

Let us now see how Raffel, with his freer hand, deals with the compounds in the passage:

> They arrived with their mail shirts
> Glittering, silver-shining links
> Clanking an iron song as they came.
> Sea-weary still, they set their broad,
> Battle-hardened shields in rows

> Along the wall, then stretched themselves
> On Herot's benches. Their armor rang.[30]

Three compounds—and the pivotal "gryregeatwum" has disappeared. So too has "hondlocen": no longer can we apprehend the toughness of the interlocked rings or of the human resolve that went into their forging—a resolve that suggests the impenetrable determination of the iron troop. Instead, we have "silver-shining," which is merely visual, and redundant after "glittering." (Also, the aural effect of this line is at odds with "clanking.") While Raffel's is an imaginative recreation of the poem, here he has failed to give the compounds their due. By simply naming the thing denoted a richness is stripped away, a violence is done to the original text. Raffel's choice is, of course, the result of the bias of modern poetry. Williams has taught us to prefer precise denotation to suggestiveness. "Swanrād" (swan's riding) is baroque periphrasis; give us the *ding an sich* instead, give us the sea itself. No. However modern his bias, the translator ought to know that to suppress the kenning and the compound is to eliminate the most distinguished feature of the poem. Tolkien sums up this issue with his typical acuity:

> It is plain that the translator dealing with these compounded words must hesitate between simply naming the thing denoted (so "harp" 1065 for "gomenwudu"—"playwood"), and resolving the combination into a phrase. The former retains compactness but loses its colour; the latter retains the colour, but even if it does not falsify or exaggerate it, it loosens and weakens the texture. One may differ in detail from the present translation, but hardly (if one respects modern as well as ancient English) in general principle: a preference for resolution.[31]

This question settled, the translator's task only begins: how indeed to translate "gyregeatwum"? While Morgan's translation demonstrates a preference for resolution, he uses an adjective phrase, "terrible in their battle-trappings"—faithful but prolix. A similar sort of loss occurs in Chickering's "fearful in war-gear"[32] and in Alexander's "in their gear of grim aspect."[33] With some luck, I hit upon "death-gear," one of the few resolved kennings I am satisfied with: to my mind, it condenses the terror evoked by this "iron troop" just as "gyregeatwum" does.

In this matter of diction, as with so much else, the translator cannot be too obliging to his modern audience. Pope found lucrative employment making Homer write couplets and wear a frock coat, but now we judge his work more Augustan than

Achaean. Some element of strangeness must be risked, suggesting the presumed archaic sounds of the old words to the original audience, as well as the darkness cast on them by the intervening centuries. The Roman and Byzantine coins recovered from Sutton Hoo were already heirlooms at the time of the ship burial: to understand their full meaning as human artifacts, we must understand their aged luster to those who laid them in the hold, as well as the tarnish that time and the earth applied to them. That is to say, the words of *Beowulf* were not young when the poet set them down—even those freshly compounded by the poet were forged from ancient elements according to the traditional formulae. The translator must contend with a double darkness and not fear to prefer that darkness to the bias his own age has for the laser-sharp light of denotation. Even though Yeats proclaimed "there's more enterprise / In walking naked," he did not forego the use of the old hieratic words, those mementos of times more heroic than the twenties and thirties. In short, some balance must be struck between the modernist temper and the ancient poet's fidelity to the decorum of tradition.

4
The Syntax of Contemplation

This chapter proves to be a miscellany of other aspects of the poem to which the translator must be attentive. Yet one unity—the poem's contemplative coloring—brings order to this miscellany. Variation, syntax, rhetorical figures, and the poem's narrative interlace are all revelatory of this, the author's essential stance toward his material.

1

Reflecting on his work, the translator of *Beowulf* is ever an apologist for inevitable loss. The poet's use of "a double or multiple statement of the same concept or idea in different words,"[1] commonly known as variation, is yet another cause of loss. Klaeber considered variation "the very soul of the Old English poetical style."[2] As Brodeur notes, variation is far more than ingenious repetition; rather, "one member of a variation may state the thought either more generally or more specifically than the other: or the second member, while restating essentially the same concept or idea, may do so in a manner which emphasizes a somewhat different aspect of it."[3] Indeed, Brodeur judges that variation plays a major role in determining the style of *Beowulf*: "Variation restrains the pace of Old English poetic narrative, gives to dialogue or monologue its leisurely or stately character, raises into high relief those concepts which the poet hopes to emphasize, and permits him to exhibit the object of his thought in all its aspects."[4] Variation gives the poem the effect of repeatedly pivoting, gazing back on what has gone before, and then moving circumspectly on. The *Beowulf* poet is a contemplative, and it is variation that reveals most fully this habit of mind. When Hrothgar inspects the rune-inscribed sword-hilt that Beowulf has retrieved from the mere, the action is suspended for a dozen lines as the poet elaborates on the meaning of that dark script:

> Hrothgar spoke—he studied the hilt,
> the old heirloom, inscribed with the beginning

The Syntax of Contemplation

of the ancient feud, when the flood, the streaming
ocean, annihilated the giant's brood,
visited them with terror.

(1687–91)

The three variations in this excerpt from the passage markedly slow its movement and create a syntactical image of the old man intently deciphering the inscription.

Variation in itself presents no difficulty for the translator: apposition, the main syntactical form for introducing variation, is still a device favored by American and English poets. But the syntactical order variation often takes in Old English is impossible to achieve in Modern English. What Leyerle calls "stylistic interlace"—"the interweaving of two or more strands of variation"[5]—can occur in Old English because of its fully developed system of inflections that grammatically reveals the relationship between any phrase or clause and the sentence in which it appears. If I translate a sample passage literally, the difficulties this poses for a translator working in an uninflected language will be apparent:

```
              Nō þaet læsest wæs
hondgemōta,        þǣr mon Hygelāc slōh,
syððan Gēata cyning      gūðe rǣsum,
frēawine folca     Frēslondum on,
Hrēðles eafora     hiorodryncum swealt,
bille gebēaten.
```
(2354b–59a)

That was not the least
of hand-to-hand meetings when one slew Higelac,
when the king of the Geats in the battle-rush,
the beloved prince of the people in Frisia,
Hrethel's son, succumbed to sword-draughts,
struck down by a blade.

Leyerle analyzes the stylistic interlace of the passage:

> *Higelac, Geata cyning, freawine folca,* and *Hrēðles* eafora make one strand; *mon . . . sloh, hiorodryncum swealt,* and *bille gebēaten* make a second strand; *þǣr, guðe rǣsum,* and *Freslondum on* make the third. The three strands are woven into a stylistic braid.[6]

The loss, in Modern English, of most of its inflections that serve as prominent syntactic markers means the translator must give up much of this interlace, or at least lose the clarity of outline of its design. Chickering, as noted before, goes the farthest of any translator in "reproducing," as he puts it, "the poetic ordering of parts, sentence by sentence."[7] But he can do so only because his translation faces the original text on the page opposite as a sort of symbiont of the text: severed from that authority, to which the reader is meant to refer constantly, the translation would be inchoate.

> Nor was it the least
> hand-to-hand combat   where Higelac lay,
> when the Geatish king,   in the fierce battle-rush
> far off in Frisia,   the friend of his people,
> Hrethel's son,   died from sword-drinks,
> struck down and slain.[8]

Though Chickering's version may strike the reader as a strange dialect of Modern English, the variation is understandable: "the Geatish king," "the friend of his people," and "Hrethel's son" are all variations of the sentence's subject, Higelac.

Donaldson's prose translation, in contrast, unbinds the variation. Trying to make an appositional structure that is clear to the reader, he lists the variations and creates redundancy: "Nor was that the least of his hand-combats when Higelac was slain, when the king of the Geats, the noble lord of his people, the son of Hrethel, died of sword-strokes in the war-storm among the Frisians, laid low by the blade."[9]

Kevin Crossley-Holland uses yet another tactic to capture the mobilelike, suspended effect of the variation; he creates a compound appositive phrase that interrupts the forward drive of the syntax in a manner similar to the Old English syntax, even though his translation does not reproduce the poet's order of the syntax:

> That grim combat
> in which Higelac was slain—Hrethel's son,
> leader of the Geats, dear lord of his people,
> struck down by swords in the bloodbath
> in Frisia—was far from the least
> of his encounters.[10]

Compared to the close-knit "stylistic braid" of the original, this is open and somewhat ungainly. The loss of inflections is the translator's stumbling block in this passage. Try as he or she might, those mobilelike structures cannot be reproduced in Modern English; in their place, strings of appositives appear, giving a clear syntax in Modern English, but too often sounding redundant rather than contemplative.

No modern version of *Beowulf,* however masterful, can register the taut, tightly interlaced structure of the poem. As Leyerle counsels, we must look to the exquisite gold and garnet artifacts of eighth century Northumbria—metal handled as if it were as biddable as cloth—for analogues of the poem's intricate artistry.[11] Coupled with that is the compression achieved partly by the poet's compounds, some of which seem to pack meaning so tightly that language is strained, as in Hopkins's fiercely "scaped" compounds. And partly achieved through the old language's system of declensions: instead of indicating grammatical relations through the morphology of his nouns and adjectives, the translator must stuff his lines with articles and prepositions, diminishing the density of the structure. I suspect that for translators of the poem in the future, Hopkins's elisions, his effort to ignore the little words of our language and move upstream against the tendencies of Modern English toward the earlier Germanic source, may prove a fruitful example:

> I am gall, I am heartburn. God's most deep decree
> Bitter would have me taste; my taste was me;
> Bones built in me, flesh filled, blood brimmed the curse.[12]

Yet Hopkins, however fine a poet he was, began no school. His eccentric syntax has proved, so far at least, a stylistic dead end.

On the other hand, given our ignorance of the exact contours of the *Beowulf* poet's language and the conventions of his art, we must assume that he manipulated the ordinary syntax of his language in a traditional manner, though with individual skill. Accordingly, I have tried to keep within the limits of Modern English syntax. I have suppressed an expected article here and there, for instance, but I believe a consistently followed principle of suppression would lead to an odd, artificial dialect few modern readers would tolerate. For similar reasons, I have used inversions sparingly and eschewed any violent disturbances of normal order:

> That was no common
> hand-combat where Higelac fell,
> after the Weder's king, beloved lord,
> Hrethel's son, in a brief skirmish
> on Frisian shores, drank his death-draught
> from an iron sword.

2

The scholarship of the past half century has given us an increasingly greater appreciation of the richness of the poem's structure—from Adeline Bartlett's seminal work, *The Larger Rhetorical Patterns in Anglo-Saxon Poetry*,[13] to Thomas Hart's more recent work on tectonic relationships in *Beowulf*.[14] Obviously, the translator must be attentive to these larger structures so that he does not lose through inadvertence an essential meaning.

Parallelism—the repeated use of corresponding syntactical forms—is, in particular, an important structural feature of the poem. Tolkien suggests that in parallelism and balance lies the structural principle of the whole poem—"it is essentially a balance, an opposition of ends and beginnings."[15] The lines themselves, he believes, "are founded on balance; an opposition between two halves of roughly equivalent phonetic weight, and significant content."[16] In this balance and opposition of the half-lines Tolkien finds "a parallel to the total structure of *Beowulf*."[17] It was, I think, the poet's vision of the mutability implicit in the mortal condition that led him to use antithesis in many of his most powerful passages. The poem's four major figures—Hrothgar, Grendel, Beowulf, and the dragon—all experience "edwendan"—a sudden reversal. Antithesis, then, seems to be at the core of the poet's idea of the structure of earthly life, as it was for the poets of the Anglo-Saxon elegies.

It should be quickly added that these four figures did not foresee the form of their sudden reversal. Life is brittle and death has sway over all, Hrothgar tells Beowulf in his great "sermon." And I think we are to infer that any of us who have had good fortune are more than a little like the foolish king Hrothgar alludes to—"the world possesses him, in his folly / he can't conceive he will ever die" (1733–34). In this way, the contemplative cast of mind turns ironic. Our wisdom consists in our knowing we have no knowledge of the shape our death will take; but the unwisdom that glosses over mortality is far more common.

Litotes, the rhetorical figure of understatement, is another index of the ironic mind, though in the case of Old English poets it might aptly be thought of as a cultural characteristic, it so permeates their work. The *Beowulf* poet is no exception—Frederick Bracher counts ninety-four uses of understatement in the poem.[18] Leech, dealing with the effects of the device in general, notes:

> Litotes expresses an overt lack of commitment, and so implies a desire to suppress or conceal one's true attitude; but paradoxically this may, like hyperbole, be a mode of intensification, suggesting that the speaker's feelings are too deep for plain expression. Because of its

two-layer significance—superficial indifference and underlying commitment—litotes is often treated as a category of irony.[19]

The effects of understatement in *Beowulf* are varied—from the poet's almost wry observation that it was not difficult to find those who sought their beds at some distance from Heorot once Grendel began visiting the hall, to his veiled acknowledgement of the intensity of Hildeburh's grief:

> Those were not spendthrift tears
> that Hoce's daughter shed, once morning came,
> the radiance of dawn, and she could see
> her murdered kinsmen, whom she had once held
> her portion of joy.
>
> (1076–80)

Taken in sum, these understatements create an effect of restraint and concealment—of griefs too large to speak and of thoughts withheld.[20] I suspect the poet did not reflect on his use of litotes; rather, like other Anglo-Saxon poets, he probably used the figure of speech unself-consciously. Like antithesis, it embodied his, and his culture's, tragic attitude toward the universe.

Considered from another vantage point, understatement implies moderation, a respect for limit, and an acceptance of man's place in the scheme of things. It also implies an attitude toward language: words, it suggests, will be taken keen note of by people and by the cosmos. A rash word might prompt a quick visitation of one sort or another. When a man makes a boast he had best be ready for action.[21] Individual words weighed more in the world of Anglo-Saxon England than they do now, and so the translator must mete them out with shrewd care. Needless to say, the translator must keep the litotes intact or he will lose a significant aspect of the poem.

3

Since the publication of Wyld's pioneering essay, "Diction and Imagery in Anglo-Saxon Poetry,"[22] Old English scholars have devoted much thought to the poet's evocative use of language and the care with which he constructs his scenes and settings. A fair-sized hedge of criticism, for instance, has grown up around Grendel's final visit to Heorot,[23] and Hrothgar's description of the mere.[24] Heorot itself has been promoted as nothing less than the "centre of the first part of the poem, the thing fought for, the exciting cause of all the action."[25]

One might ponder with profit, in the manner of Auerbach, the techniques the poet uses to represent reality. While Heorot is not laid open to the reader's gaze as Tolstoy, or another realist, would represent it, the precise lineaments of the hall, from the scar on Unferth's cheek, say, to the gold thread worked into Freyja's gown, as she was imaged in the tapestry hanging behind Hrothgar's high seat, etc., the hall nonetheless has discrete features—it is high and horn-gabled (82), decorated with jewels (167), gold-adorned (308); it is reinforced, inside and out, with iron bands (773–75), and has benches inlaid with gold (775–76). Within, the great ceremonies are held, oaths are made, and gold bestowed; the human light is kindled; Grendel, creature of darkness, pollutes the fair house, gloats and fattens on human flesh; there, Beowulf receives a hero's wage and Wealtheow moves about, bearing the golden cup, encouraging her sons, making her speeches like charms against the coming fire. All is stylized, intricate, ceremonial: the poet grants us to see just what is essential to comprehend the grandeur of Heorot and the horror of Grendel. Bartlett has likened *Beowulf* to a tapestry, and the metaphor is illuminating:

> I believe that the method of *Beowulf* is the method of all Anglo-Saxon epic; and I should prefer to characterize it as a tapestry, which presents its pictures in a series of panels. Each verse pattern is a panel or section of the storied tapestry. It has an organic unity of its own and it also has its place in the series of pictures (some of them narrative, some descriptive, some didactic) which tells a connected, unified story. At any given moment the poet may appear to be more interested in the elaborate detail than in the composition of the whole. Still, his panels fit smoothly as a rule into a reasonably harmonious scheme of presentation; the tapestry is an integrated and generally consistent piece of work.[26]

Contemplating this "storied tapestry," the translator learns a keen respect for the integrity of each scene and setting; the poet provides enough detail to create an imaginative space for the mind, enthralled by the story, to move through. Enough and no more: we are to view the tapestry, as did the poet his material, from some distance. As Brodeur acknowledges, the poet likes to contemplate the "typical aspects"[27] of things—the qualities of a king or a good sword, but not the specific and especially not the idiosyncratic. The poet's vision is gnomic as well as ironic. Even when the focus is tight, as when Grendel snatches up the hapless Geat and gobbles him down "fet ond folma" (740–45), or Hrothgar studies the sword-hilt (1687–99), the frame is wide: it is Everyman, or, at least, an average Geat warrior, whom Grendel devours; on the hilt is engraved, apparently, a verse or two from one of the chapters of Genesis.

These are effects that touch on the topology of cultures. The poet sees his characters *sub specie aeternitatis*, in their static and eternal lineaments. Memory, and his identity as a Christian poet meditating on human destiny, permit him this distance. As the poet makes, he contemplates. As I have noted, the device of variation embodies the motion of turning something over in the mind and pondering its essential attributes; it is, in other words, a form of contemplation. This, for Ananda Coomaraswamy, was one of the defining qualities of the medieval artist:

> The man incapable of contemplation cannot be an artist, but only a skilful workman; it is demanded of the artist to be both a contemplative and a good workman. Best of all if, like the angels, he need not in his activity "lose the delights of inward contemplation."[28]

The *Beowulf* poet has a contemplative attitude toward his material, shaping and disposing it so that his reader may contemplate it as well. But how does the translator handle this "contemplative coloring" of the poem?

To begin with, he uses the sort of diction I argue for in the previous chapter; the language chosen must have some measure of formality, the words must have some weight and some patina. Likewise, the words must express the same level of generality as the original word—to use a too highly denotative language is to be familiar with the original material in a way the poet was not. The inside of Heorot must not be presented too precisely, the mere must remain half-concealed. Almost all of the translators of *Beowulf* have realized this, yet it goes against the modern grain always to stay at the level of the typical, the suggestive. Raffel, in keeping with his modernist aesthetic of translation, permits himself the liberty of reaching toward the particular, inventing, for instance, Gothic effects to describe the mere:

> They live in secret places, windy
> Cliffs, wolf-dens where water pours
> From the rocks, then runs underground, where mist
> Steams like black clouds, and the groves of trees
> Growing out over their lake are all covered
> With frozen spray, and wind down snakelike

> Roots that reach as far as the water
> And help keep it dark.[29]
>
> (1358–65)

There are no "black clouds," no "snakelike roots" winding down in the original. Raffel seeks his modern audience too solicitously, casting too sharp a light on the mere. Morgan preserves the mere's strangeness in his more faithful version:

> It is not far distant
> Measured in miles that that lake lies,
> Groves overhang it clothed in hoarfrost,
> A great rooted wood throws shade on its water.[30]
>
> (1361–64)

This is a "dygel lond" (1357): to describe it too precisely betrays its secrecy.

I have noted that Modern English has a bias toward precision that Old English does not share. Raffel speaks of diving into the Old English until he has it "at his finger tips" and then emerging, leaving the Old English behind, and making his way "into modern English poetry."[31] He argues that the translator must be "free to *create* in the new linguistic medium."[32] This freedom has enabled him to produce a vigorous, modern translation, or imitation, of *Beowulf*. By using brusque enjambments and suppressing the variation, he achieves an energetic style. This is not entirely alien to the poem, for the old poet often ends his verse sentences in the middle of the line and so hauls the reader onward with the alliteration commencing the next verse sentence. But Raffel's version underplays the poem's contemplativeness: the gnomic pauses, the delays of variation, the dense, sometimes irreversibly bonded compounds that, I suspect, were meant to be savored by the original audience and not quickly resolved into their supposed referents. The unfolding of the plot indeed provides an excitement that draws the reader on, but along the way the reader should not lose "the delights of inward contemplation."

I do not suggest the poem is merely a machine to exercise the Anglo-Saxon's extraordinary capacity for contemplation. The poem tastes of life, however much idealized, and nowhere is that more apparent than in the character's speeches. Recent criticism has shown how alive these speeches are to the nuances of the dramatic situation.[33] Consider Beowulf's reply to Unferth's insinuations that Breca proved himself superior to Beowulf. The speech begins brusquely enough with an insult and a short sentence, which, one can well imagine, was said with some heat. Quickly (532–34), he defends himself in another brusque sentence and makes his boast. Then Beowulf recounts his version of the Breca episode, and we hear the voice become quieter and more reflective as he remembers and gives himself over to the telling of the story. This telling rises to a climax with the hieratic and magnificent, "Lēoht ēastan cōm, / beorht bēacen Godes, brimu swaþredon, / þæt ic sǣnæssas gesēon mihte / windige weallas" (569–72) ("Light came from the east, / God's bright beacon, the water grew wondrous calm / so that I saw windy sea-walls, / and steep headlands."). And that, in turn, is followed by the almost impenetrable gnome, "Wyrd oft nereð / unfǣgne eorl, þonne his ellen dēah" (572–73) ("Fate often spares / the man unmarked by death if his courage holds."). This requires diction of a loftier register and phrasing of a nobler cadence than the blunt and colloquial opening of the speech. At line 583, Beowulf's speech takes an abrupt turn back to the informal, heated voice with "Nō ic wiht fram þē. . . ." The reader may imagine the hero has stirred himself from his reveries and now fixes Unferth with a baleful eye. His dramatic telling, interrupted by gnomic statements and light imagery suggestive of God's intercession, gives force to his biting condemnation of Unferth's prowess. Beowulf concludes the speech with a second boast and pledge, and a typically ambiguous prediction, which is something like a blend between a gnome, a boast, and a knocking on wood: "Gǣþ eft sē þe mōt / tō medo mōdig, siþþan morgenlēoht / ofer ylda bearn ōþres dōgores, / sunne sweglwered sūþan scīneð!" (603–6) ("Let him who may / go blithe to drink when the morning light / of another day—the sun through radiant cloud— / shines from the south over the sons of men."). The language here rises again into the formal register. Such swift modulations of tone and passion characterize many of the speeches in the poem. Given the stiff harness of the poet's form, they represent an achievement comparable to Shakespeare's handling of the sonnet: both poets "sing in their chains" so well we understand that form is no encumbrance to them.

Clearly, the translator must attempt to represent this modulation—the rapid changes in mood, the shifts of diction—and yet not forego all formality and form. The translator, for many reasons, cannot, and probably should not, bind his lines so tightly as the poet. Raffel, for instance, achieves an admirable, if rather free, version of the opening of Beowulf's speech:

> "Ah! Unferth, my friend, your face
> Is hot with ale, and your tongue has tried
> To tell us about Brecca's doings. But the truth
> Is simple: no man swims in the sea
> As I can, no strength is a match for mine."[34]

As usual, Raffel has allowed himself a long tether, but the lines move well, are basically four-stress, and are loosely alliterated. The voice is alive and believable. It is no easy task to write lines that seem to breathe with a human breath, and yet obey formal constraints.

Beyond what I've said here, is it the translator's task at all to consider the larger structures as they work in *Beowulf*? Chickering likens "the limit of our aural attention" to the "rectangular frame of the camera or the circle of light from a flashlight moving down the page"—a swatch of light "which has to move if we are to see the next thing that happens."[35] Similarly, the translator creeps through the text: a single word like "weorodrǣdende" ("woroldrǣdenne"?) or "unhlitme"—to choose only two from the unusually opaque Finn episode—may stop him dead in his tracks for a day or two. Indeed, at times it seems to the translator that he gropes through an impenetrable darkness with the pencil beam of a flashlight.

Though he does seem to dawdle, ruminating on the matter of his story as he goes along, the poet pulls the translator forward through the links of alliteration, the enjambments, the ring structures. His poem seems utterly purposive. Far from conceiving the poem as a patchwork pagan text, quilted over and corrupted by meddling Christian clerks, the *Beowulf* scholar is beginning to conjecture a work of intricate interlace and mathematical unity.[36] It is rather as if an archaeologist uncovers what he first believes to be a bronze-age burial mound that, on further excavation, begins to suggest the lineaments and symmetry of a cathedral.

It is not in the translator's jurisdiction to submit a theory of the poem's structure or to refashion the poem according to his own conception of its shape, omitting those lines he considers scribal interpolations, paring away the excess tissue that blurs the contours of "his" version of the text. The poem must be seen whole. For instance, what many have deemed the poet's weakness—his tendency to sermonize—I find one of his strengths. As moderns we are taught to loathe didacticism, but the poet loves nothing better than a well-turned gnomic saying.

So, line by line, the translator assays the echoing labyrinth, attempting to remember the way he has come so he can mark the resonance of a recurring motif. The burial of Beowulf, for instance, causes the translator to gaze back on the setting adrift of Scyld's funeral ship, and that in turn recalls the mysterious arrival of Scyld from the sea. Blomfield notes: "Not by transitions and transformations but by suggestion of the ever-present identity of seed in fruit and fruit in seed does the poet adjust the emotional tension."[37] In this largest motion, the poet encompasses the beginning and the end of the Scyldings and the Geats—from the vantage point of the poet, the tribes' histories are as complete as the life cycle of an extinct species. It is all past, all memory. And the poet makes no attempt to have his audience experience that history as anything but finished story. He records the building of Heorot and in his next breath foretells its destruction by fire; he grimly demonstrates Grendel's cruel strength and in his next breath intimates the demon has met his match in the hero's handgrip. A strong determination operates in *Beowulf:* as fate governs the affairs of the Anglo-Saxons, so memory governs the events of the poem.

The poet has been handed his story in a particular form: Klaeber comments that the historical elements have "an air of reality and historical truth about them which is quite remarkable."[38] Klaeber is not willing to grant the "frankly fabulous matter of preternatural character" equal verisimilitude; but the reader must concede that it is handled with all the dignity and seriousness given the "historical elements."[39] Though our credulity may flag, the poet's does not. The monsters are also part of the given of the story, the given that the poet has to work with and embellish, but not alter.

Klaeber could not rid himself of the notion that a contest with a demon or a dragon is a theme unworthy of an epic. The poet, obviously, did not think so, nor can the translator afford such incredulity. The constraints lie even more heavily on him than on the poet: often he is handling material he only half understands. Ignorance, if not a sense of fidelity to the original, compels him to toe the line. The poet handles the dragon like a fact of nature, not a supernatural visitant; the translator must do the same. This applies equally to the so-called digressions: we are subjecting the poem to an alien code of conscience to ask that it possess a linear, Aristotelian unity. Leyerle has shown us how to begin to view the poem as analogous in structure to the interlaced carpet pages of the Lindisfarne Gospels: "An episode cannot be taken out of context . . . without impairing the interwoven design."[40] He concludes emphatically: "There are no digressions in *Beowulf*."[41] The translator must accept that as a governing assumption.

Any large-scale literary work out of the ancient past must strike us as a kind of memory because it has preserved what otherwise had been lost. Preeminently, *The Iliad* and *The Odyssey* are such works; *Beowulf* is a third. I have noted the structures that make it, literally, mnemonic. The narrative interlace is yet another. The poet does not work according to the Aristotelian logic of temporal sequence, but by the associative connections of memory. *Beowulf* is not simply the story of one hero, his early triumph and "his inevitable overthrow in Time,"[42] but rather it is a heroic memory, what has been remembered of two interlinked tribes, the Geats and the Scyldings. At the same time, it is a contemplation of that memory, providing the modern reader, as it did its original audience, with a large and generous understanding of his, and his civilization's, place in time.

5
The Act of Translation

In this chapter, I will discuss my handling of three passages from *Beowulf*, attempting to give an accurate image of how I went about the task of translation. Such remembered recreations of a process are inevitably false to a degree; the reader should keep in mind the inspired legerdemain of Poe's recipe for "The Raven." The following is not submitted as an exact mirroring of my hermeneutic method, but rather as a fairly reliable map of the route I took—the books I consulted, the dictionaries, articles, and notes read, the paths tried but found impassable (recalling the child's game of reaching the castle within the hindering maze—the erratic journey traced by the uncertain pencil lead), the fortunate illuminations and bewildering marshlights, the deceptively sure-footed final version, striding all too confidently down the page. The reader may expect to learn how I made my way, my characteristic method of advancing over rough terrain.

It may also seem at times that I have abandoned the principles set forth in the previous chapters or at least that I have applied them inconsistently. The reader who wishes to find a close fit between this chapter and the previous chapters will be disappointed; but, as I indicated in the first chapter, theory can give the translator only a general instrument for finding the way. Sometimes, as I expected, the imaginative grasp of a single line demanded an unpremeditated solution—as surprising to the translator as to the reader. For the translator is that queer, amphibious creature, part scholar, part artist, who must know when a fuller collaboration with the text requires a departure from the text or at the least a more relaxed enforcement of his carefully formulated principles.

Yet those principles do provide a framework for the translator's work. The four-stress line, the diction of a higher tone, the resolution of kennings into phrases, the fidelity to the rhetorical figures and to the contemplative character of the poem—these represent controlling biases that informed my choices, providing the work as a whole with a unity it would not have otherwise possessed.

1

Among the glories of *Beowulf* are its passages of dialogue. These vary immensely in character, from the ceremonial speeches of Wealhtheow (cf. 1216–31) to the boasts of the proud young Beowulf (cf. 555–58). Often they are woven of several emotional strands, as is the case with Beowulf's reply to Unferth. In the space of a dozen lines, Beowulf moves from a grim joke about the sea-beasts' spoiled banquet on the ocean bottom (562–67) through the triumphant image of God's beacon light showing him cliffs and headlands (569–72) to the austere and impersonal gnome, "Wyrd oft nereð / unfægne eorl þonne his ellen dēah" ("Fate often spares / the man unmarked by death if his courage holds"). The translator of such a speech must transmit rapid motions of thought and feeling, and yet give an overarching unity to the voice.

Though it would be instructive to analyze my handling of Beowulf's entire speech, its length prohibits that. Instead, I will focus on the opening of Unferth's challenge to Beowulf—lines 506–15.

The interpretation of the character of Unferth—his role in the Danish court and his function in the poem—is itself a crux. Much of the critical commentary centers on the meaning of the unusual word, "þyle," applied to Unferth. Klaeber's glosses of "orator," "spokesman," "official entertainer," sum up his idea of the "þyle"; he endorses the view that "the characteristics of his office seem to have been 'age, wisdom, extended knowledge, and a seat of honor' (Larson)."[1] More recently, critics have doubted the dignity of the "þyle" and glossed the word as "scurrilous jester."[2] Others, leaning hard on interpretations of the meaning of ON "þulr," believe it should be translated, "heathen priest,"[3] possibly one with strong fealty to Odin.[4] Carol Clover sets the episode squarely in the Germanic flyting tradition: she suggests Unferth is doing Hrothgar good service by testing the bold young newcomer. Far from being an eruption of violent bad manners, Unferth's speech may be viewed as proper etiquette.[5] Thus Unferth may be seen as the initiator of a lying match, a match in which Beowulf participates with gusto and imagination, or as the haughty and powerful challenger of the daring stranger in Hrothgar's court.

Either conception of "þyle" will, of course, issue in different readings of the "Unferth Intermezzo" and, indeed, of much of the action at Hrothgar's court. My own study of the text, especially of Unferth's speech, leads me to judge Unferth to be a fierce and fully serious power at the court.

In his introduction to the speech, the poet makes clear how we are to read Unferth's lines. They constitute his "beadurūne" (501)—his "battle-rune," his words of insult and challenge. The poet tells us that Unferth is jealous of Beowulf's undertaking (501-2) because he cannot bide the fact that any man might enjoy more fame than he himself (503-5). In a play, such an introduction might call for the stage direction, *spoken with venom* or *spleen*. We expect insult and that is precisely what we get.

Unferth's ploy is dialectically brilliant: his opening question, ostensibly to establish Beowulf's identity, is an accusation and an indictment of Beowulf's good judgment and character:

"Eart þū sē Bēowulf,   sē þe wið Brecan wunne,
on sīdne sæ   ymb sund flite,
ðær git for wlence   wada cunnedon
ond for dolgilpe   on dēop wæter
aldrum nēþdon?   Nē inc ænig mon,
nē lēof nē lāð,   belēan mihte
sorhfullne sīð,   þā git on sund rêon;
þær git ēagorstrēam   earmum þehton,
mæton merestræta,   mundum brugdon,
glidon ofer gārsecg. . . ."

(506-15a)

"Eart þū sē Bēowulf"—"Are you that Beowulf"—insolently implying that there might be more than one Beowulf and knowing full well this is the one and only, Unferth begins. The interpretation of the line presents no difficulties: "winnan" is a frequently used verb meaning "to strive, contend, fight."[6] The pronouns are unambiguous, the preposition "wið" in this passage has very much the same meaning it presently has in collocation with verbs of contending or combating. Indeed, we might say exactly the same thing today: "Are you that Beowulf who struggled with Breca?" Scorn still accents *that*.

Line 507 is not so transparent. "Sīdne sæ" presents no problems; it is a common collocation, a formula, in Old English poetry[7] (cf. "Christ I," 1.852) that came ready enough to the poet's hand. But the translator must mark it as the first of Unferth's many allusions to the sea, allusions that the poet uses to good effect. "Sund" here is not the "sea," but, rather, "the act of swimming."[8] Interestingly, the translator comes on the following quotation from "The Second Dialogue of Solomon and Saturn" under the definition of "sund" meaning the "power of swimming": "Dol bið se þe gæð on deop wæter / se þe sund nafað. . . ." (47–48).[9] It is as if the poet self-consciously echoes this passage, which is phrased as a "wisdom" utterance, given the several words it shares with the lines under scrutiny. "Flitan" occurs infrequently in Old English texts and means, according to Bosworth and Toller, to "strive, contend, rebel."[10] Curiously, it also occurs in the opening lines of "Solomon and Saturn"—"Hwæt, ic flitan gefræn on fyrndagum"—implying here a fierce intellectual engagement.[11] The verb is also used, in participial form, in line 916 ("Hwīlum flītende fealwe strǣte / mēarum mǣton") in reference to the impromptu horse races inspired by Beowulf's victory. I read it as an intensive word, referring to an especially vigorous contest. Unferth may be implying here what he makes explicit in the next two lines—that the two undertook the contest out of foolish pride.

"Wlenco" in *Beowulf*, has sharply contrasting meanings. In line 328, "wlenco" is used in its positive sense, "pride, as in high spirits."[12] Hrothgar observes that Beowulf has come to the aid of his father's old ally because of his "wlenco." But in this passage the meaning is negative (as in line 1206 when Beowulf says that Higelac raided Frisia for "wlenco"). "Superbia" would probably be a fair gloss. The Old English moralists made clear their feelings about this word; in passage after passage, "wlenc" refers to the pomp and vanity of mutable, earthly things.

"Dolgilpe" is a *hapax legomenon*, compounded from "dol and "gilp." "Dol" is another of those words Christian moralists were so fond of: "Dol bið se þe him his dryhten ne ondrǣdeð; to þæs oft cymeð dead unþinged,"[13] a sentiment the *Beowulf* poet would readily endorse. It means "foolish, erring, heretical."[14] "Gilp" is an ambivalent word like "wlenco"—it may mean "ostentation, pride, arrogance, boast, or glory."[15] Here the context, as well as the first element of the compound, limits the meaning. "Dolgilpe" thus means something like "foolish boast" or "reckless pride." Grendel, we have just learned, is a "dolsceaða" whom God will take care of.

Unferth, however, does more than characterize Beowulf as a man guilty of overweening pride; through alliteration and syntax, these qualities are yoked to the deeds that Breca and Beowulf attempt: "ðǣr git for wlence wada cunnedon / ond for dolgilpe on dēop wæter / aldrum nēþdon?" The syntax suggests the mortal recklessness of their undertaking—"wlence" is balanced with the "wada" ("waters") that the two make trial of; "dolgilpe" is balanced with the "dēop wæter" on which the two risk their lives. That linking might well serve to intensify the dramatic audience's sense of the adventure's foolhardiness. It is a strategy Unferth will continue to use.

In the next independent clause (510b–12b), Unferth establishes the pair's headstrong nature. (We remember Unferth's words when Higelac chides Beowulf for ignoring his counsel.) The clause is short and straightforward with a single variation on "mon" ("nē lēof nē lað"). That variation appears to be a conventional collocation, like "young and old," "rich and poor," but does not occur elsewhere in Old English poetry. "Belēan" seems to be an emphatic word meaning "hinder by blame, reprehend, forbid"; like "dol" it is also favored by the Christian homilists.[17] "Reôn" (512) is an unusual word. Wrenn notes that the use of "rowan" to mean "swim" only occurs in *Beowulf*.[18] Its more conventional meaning is "to row" or "to sail"; yet the extension of meaning is unremarkable. When translating "sorhfullne," the writer must keep in mind that "sorh" has a larger, more varied meaning than Modern English "sorrow." It may mean pain or trouble also. "Sīð" too is a word rich in meaning—"journey, death, expedition, enterprise, road, occasion" are all synonyms Clark Hall lists.[19] The translator needs to consider what "sīð" might mean in personal terms to the Anglo-Saxon—a hard journey of the sort dramatized in "The Seafarer," ending, perhaps, in exile. In this passage the meaning is nearest "journey" or "adventure." It should be noted that the next appearance of "sīð," at line 765b, refers to Grendel's final "sīð" to Heorot, significantly, a "gēocor" (a "bitter" or "sad") "sīð."

The passage's salient stylistic feature is its variation of "sǣ"—the next three lines have four such variations. Through them, Unferth continues and intensifies his strategy of establishing Beowulf's extraordinary foolhardiness. These variations are words of great dignity and ancientness that suggest the sea's venerable power. On the other hand, the actions that Unferth attributes to the swimmers might be considered objective correlatives of "dolgilpe."

"Ēagorstrēam," the passage's other *hapax legomenon*, compounded of "eagor" and "strēam," seems like one of those words sprung from the race's memory. "Ēagor" is cognate with ON *ægir*, which, Cleasby writes, "is an old mythical word, the root of which is not to be sought for in the Norse languages, for it is much older; it may be akin to the Gr. Okeanos, both being derived from some Indo-European root."[20] "Strēam," a less ancient word, means "current, flowing water."[21] While it is not, technically, incorrect to translate "ēagorstrēam" as "ocean-current" or "sea-stream," it is a palpable loss. Only by grasping the archaic and mythical dimensions of the word can the full irony of the swimmers' actions ("earmum þehton") be appreciated—"þeccean" means "to cover an object with something."[22] Surely Unferth is mocking the swimmers who thought to cover with their arms the unsayably vast and ancient sea-streams.

Another possibly comic image of hubris is "mǣton merestrǣta." "Metan" means to "measure by paces" and "traverse."[23] "Merestrǣta" occurs in only one other place in Old English poetry, "Elene" (242);[24] Klaeber gives its meaning as "sea-path."[25] Again, I suspect Unferth is ridiculing the swimmers by suggesting the enormous disparity between the human hands that would do the measuring and the endless streets of the sea. The next half line continues the effect—"brugdon" is the preterite third person plural of "bregdan," which Bosworth and Toller translates as "to vibrate" in this passage.[26] The image, I think, is meant to suggest the contrast between the minute, flurried human activity and the calm immensity of the ocean, an image Unferth concludes with "glidon ofer gārsecg." "Glidon" is one of those dependable words that a millenium has left little mark on: it means "they glided."[27] "Gārsecg," on the other hand, is a kenning for sea with a provenance, I suspect, fully as ancient as that of "ēagorstrēam." It means, literally, "spear-man." Bosworth and Toller note that it refers to "the myth of the armed man" associated with the sea, probably bearing some "analogy to the personification of Neptune,"[28] though Derolez shows just how problematic the word's meaning is.[29] "Glidon ofer gārsecg" may also have held some comic incongruity for the original audience.

This interpretation of lines 513–15 is, admittedly, speculative. It would fit well with the insulting tone Unferth establishes in the first few lines of his speech. Indeed, Unferth seems to speak more like a Christian homilist than a priest of Odin, an appropriate anachronism. While unprovable, this reading is the result of a close engagement with the text and a contemplation of individual words. For a dead language like Old English, a language with a small preserved literature, this act of contemplation is beset with perils. No doubt a resurrected Anglo-Saxon would find delightful howlers in the most erudite and circumspect of translations. And the translator, while availing himself of the scholar's labors, must, for the sake of his work's vitality, rely on his intuitions as well as his Bosworth and Toller. Indeed it is risky to conjecture that irony which, I believe, give these lines their bite. It could be an artifact, but for the translator to reject such a reading, safely opting for a neutral reading, creates a neutral, if not neutered, translation.

We have then a literal version:

> Are you that Beowulf who with Breca contended,
> on the broad sea concerning swimming competed,
> where you two for pride of waters made trial
> and for foolish-boast on deep water
> lives risked? Not you two any man
> neither beloved or loathed, dissuade could
> from grievous adventure, when you two on sea swam;
> there you two sea-streams with arms covered,
> measured sea-streets, with hands vibrated,
> glided over spear-man.

I quickly turned this into the following "first working":

Are you that Beowulf who contended with Breca
in a swimming match on the broad sea
where you two for pride made trial of the sea
and out of foolish boasting risked your very lives
in the deep sea? Nor any man, neither friend nor foe,
could dissuade you two
from the perilous adventure, when you set out on the sea.
There you two covered the sea-streams with your arms, swept quickly with your hands,
glided over the spear-man.

Now the hard part. I glance over a draft streaked with erasures, crammed with lines crossed out, words pencilled in, uncertainly, at the margins—the rough record of what was primarily a long session of reading and rereading the original, muttering the lines out loud, and then listening to my tentative equivalents, trying out lines and discarding them even before I set them down.

Line 506, as I have written, offered little resistance. Line 507 was much harder. Already, in the first working, I took liberties, translating "ymb sund flite" into "swimming contest." That version, however, was both awkward and limp. I wanted it to have some of the energy and crisp movement achieved by the assonance of the *is*. Thus: "risked the sea in a swimming match" seemed fairly accurate in its movement, sound, and meaning.

But I really took the plunge in the next two lines. A straightforward version, as in my first working, struck me as inadequate. It did not capture the braiding of "wlence" and "wada," "dolgilpe" and "dēop." Because I judge braiding to be an especially significant stylistic feature, generating much of the passage's meaning, I translated what I considered that meaning to be: because of their pride and their reckless boasts, the men are yoked to the "wada" and the "dēop wæter." Thus: "where towering pride and reckless vaunt / placed you in harness to the waves themselves / and the fathomless water." The direct translation of "aldrum nēþdon" is lost, yet the meaning is certainly there to the inferring mind.

My first assay of the next verse was again much more faithful (in the superficial sense) than the second version I settled on: "No man, / neither friend nor foe, could dissuade you / from the dismal enterprise when you put to sea." Clearly this was a weakening of the first version. I tried a freer version: "could change your mind— / you were dead-set on suffering the sea's will." No go: I had broken too far away from the original sense. Yet "dissuade" was too weak an equivalent of "belēan." I sought stronger alternatives; "could curb the folly / of your setting forth alone and on the sea" and "could keep you from the folly. . . ." "Alone" is indefensible, yet I felt I needed it rhythmically. I liked the tightness of "curb the folly," yet I chose, after some self-argument, "could keep you from the folly" because it sounded more natural to my ear. Unferth, as I conceived him, would be more likely to say that. Either way, I left the literal behind. Both "belēan mihte" and "sorhfullne sīð," along with the judgment implicit in "dolgilpe" and "for wlence," suggested the more explicit phrasing of my version.

All this might well make the scholar turn away in distaste from the impressionistic enterprise of translation. Why add "alone" if it is not there, he may ask. This is very like the microscopist who has hovered over his ocular too long and so represents his paramecium with a flagellum when it has none. "Alone" and much else is false: a mere artifact of the translator's errant mind.

His reply must be, "For the sake of imaginative truth, for the more accurate music of the line, for the echo of 'rêon' in 'alone.' For the spirit and not the literal, inanimate letter." And yet, of course, in the name of "spirit," a great travesty and betrayal might be carried out. The outcome of the whole game depends, finally, on the tact and accuracy of the translator's intuitions.

This exculpatory aside is meant to introduce a liberty that makes the addition of "alone" the least of venial sins. Lines 513–15a are masterly: the poet granted Unferth a brilliant rhetorical effect. By balancing, on one side of the caesura, the ancient "ēagorstrēam," a name of patina and great age, even for the poet's contemporaries, with the rapid movement of the foolish mortals' tiny hands and arms, he satirizes Beowulf and Breca and suggests the enormity of their *hubris*. To register this effect, I needed to discover some equally striking image of *hubris*.

And so the substance of these two and a half lines undergoes a sea-change indeed. "Gārsecg" became "ancient mother," which, I think, is nearer our culture's sense of the sea as the cradle of life and genetrix. ("Spearman" would mean nothing to the contemporary reader and "sea" would not mean enough.) The first element of the variation, "ēagorstrēam," became an attribute of "ancient mother"—her "winding currents." The compound, "merestrǣta," disappeared, with my regrets, under the verge. The two parallel phrases, "earmum þehton" and "mundum brugdon," suggested the half-line, "thinking to measure." "Glidon ofer gārsecg" underwent the most remarkable metamorphosis: it became the appositive clause, "flyspecks on her expanse"—flyspecks, indeed, the scholar might interject, on the translator's bifocals. Yet the phrase suggests the vast and comic discrepancy between the two swimmers and the sea they assayed. Beowulf himself as much as admits that it was a foolish adventure and so exonerates himself by claiming both he and Breca were young boys when they undertook the "sīð" (535–38).

This is my final version of the passage:

> Are you that Beowulf who struggled with Breca,
> risked the sea in a swimming match
> where towering pride and reckless vaunt
> placed you in harness to the waves themselves
> and the fathomless water? No man,
> neither friend nor foe, could keep you from the folly
> of setting forth alone, and on the sea.
> There you two were on the ancient mother,
> thinking to measure her winding currents,
> flyspecks on her expanse.

This, in brief, represents my own work with a short passage—my wrestling with the ambiguities, especially, of individual words and my efforts to transmit not only the literal, surface meaning (if such a meaning can be said to exist) but also the implications of syntax and sound, and the imagined inflections of Unferth's voice. I read Unferth's speech as a passionate, satiric attack on Beowulf's heroic reputation and so I attempted to convey that savage indignation in my version. But his speech, as has been seen, is not crude ridicule: Unferth is canny and impugns Beowulf for precisely that quality for which all heroes are suspect, *hubris*. Unferth comes across as a shrewd homilist, and so, along with the spleen, I have sought to invest him with some dignity.

2

There is a *tristesse* that overtakes the translator of *Beowulf*, a feeling that must be like the poet's own regard for those rusted helms and breast-plates Wiglaf discovers in the dragon's barrow. While the translator, in an idle moment, may imagine himself a sort of Last Survivor standing between the poem and the future when all keys of remembrance are lost, in bleaker moments he sees himself as a sexton toiling in a boneyard of dead words and forgotten legends, exhuming their shattered torsos with no clear idea of how to articulate them. Then the translator is poignantly aware of that ghostly audience, the poet's collaborators, whose experience of the world and whose memories of his people's stories linked with the poem and made it whole. No polisher, no "feormynd," can step forth from that ghostly audience and restore the lines to their former luster.

Every line of the poem implies that spectral audience, but few sections to such a degree as the "Finnsburg Episode" (1069–1159). The dramatic audience—the Danes and the Geats inside Heorot—and, presumably, the audience for which the poet wrote, were insiders, privy to just that knowledge which makes this section slippery with allusiveness to the modern reader:

> The allusiveness in question is of a very concentrated kind, i.e. it does not go outside the matter in hand; it is solely to personages and events contained in the story. That is obviously an allusiveness which the teller can only permit himself when the story is not a new one, when he reckons on its already being known to his audience. But the poet sang for his contemporaries, not for us, and we no longer know what was familiar to everybody in those days. The allusiveness is therefore attended by *our* ignorance. Again, it is the main events, a clear statement of which would be necessary to *us*, if we were immediately to grasp the story, which are conveyed thus allusively. That is to say, the poet is *not*, in the ordinary meaning of the word, *telling* a story, i.e. narrating a chain of happenings in the order in which they occurred. He is rather recalling to his hearers' minds well-known situations which could be conjured up by merely alluding to well-known events and personages.[30]

In reading the "Finnsburg Fragment" and the "Finnsburg Episode," we are intensely conscious of being outsiders: we have no

The Act of Translation 71

idea whether it was Finn who ambushed Hnæf or if the "eotena" (the Jutes?) among Finn's retinue stirred up the quarrel and Finn was reluctantly drawn in. We only know the outcome: Finn cannot dislodge Hengest and his band from the hall and so must accept a most dissatisfying peace. Finn and Hengest are yoked together by a bitter truce, and Finn must be a ring-giver to those men whose prince he has killed—surely a sour irony for both Finn and Hengest.

To demonstrate how I handled the "Finnsburg Episode," I've selected lines 1125–31a. It is neither the most transparent nor the most difficult of the passages in the episode. But it does present textual problems of a major sort. Unpunctuated (as it appears in the original manuscript) but arranged in lines (as the original is not), the text is as follows:

>   Gewiton him ðā wīgend   wīca nēosian
>   frēondum befeallen   Frȳsland gesēon
>   hāmas ond hēaburh   Hengest ðā gȳt
>   wælfāgne winter   wunode mid finnel
>   ... unhlitme   eard gemunde
>   þeah þe he meahte   on mere drifan
>   hringedstefnan[31]

The most striking textual difficulty here is the "finnel / unhlitme." Clearly, it is a transcription error, but of what? Examining the variant emendations proposed, Dobbie reasons thus:

> The MS. *mid finnel unhlitme*, which is deficient as regards both sense and meter, has been variously emended. Kemble (2ed.) read *mid Finne* as the end of l. 1128, and so most later edd. This leaves the -l of the MS. *finnel* to be explained, as well as the word *unhlitme*, which is apparently an adverb. Kemble (2ed.) read *elne unhlitme* as l. 1129a (probably on the model of l. 1097a) and so Holder (2ed.), Socin (6,7 ed.), Holthausen (1–5, 7ed.), Schucking and Chambers. Heyne and Socin (5ed.) read *ealles unhlitme;* Klaeber, Holthausen (6,8 ed.) and von Schaubert read *eal unhlitme*.[32]

Dobbie's is the majority opinion in this matter; Donald Fry, in his 1974 edition of the "Episode,"[33] and Chickering, in his 1977 edition of *Beowulf*,[34] both agree with him, at least regarding the emendation.

A second emendation has usually been made at line 1130a: "þeah þe he *ne* meahte."[35] Fry, in his rather eccentric handling of this passage, argues at some length that Anglo-Saxons could sail in winter and thus leaves the text unemended.[36] Of course, it may be

72   Commentary

that it was not the ice-locked waters but Hengest's oath that compelled him to stay. In any case, leaving the line as it is seems to make the imagery of the frozen winter seas an unnecessary ornament. Fry has also punctuated the passage in a maverick way:

>   Gewiton him ða wigend   wica neosian
>   freondum befeallen,   Frysland geseon.
>   Hamas and hea-burh   Hengest ða gyt
>   wælfagne winter   wunode mid Finne
>   eal unhlitme   (eard gemunde),
>   þeah þe he meahte   on mere drifan
>   hringed-stefnan.³⁷

Usually, "hamas ond hea-burh" have been seen to belong to the previous verse sentence, and a period has been placed after "eal unhlitme."³⁸ "Eard gemunde" has been seen as the independent clause in the succeeding complex sentence and not as a parenthetical insertion. Klaeber, Dobbie, and Chickering all agree on how the passage ought to be emended and punctuated:

>   Gewiton him ðā wīgend   wīca nēosian
>   frēondum befeallen,   Frȳsland gesēon,
>   hāmas ond hēaburh.   Hengest þā gȳt
>   wælfāgne winter   wunode mid Finne
>   [ea]l unhlitme   eard gemunde,
>   þeah þe *ne* meahte   on mere drīfan
>   hringedstefnan.

This is the textual interpretation that I have worked from. It is speculative, of course, but the agreement of three such capable scholars ought to give the translator some confidence for undertaking the next stage of his work.

I worked through the passages with Bosworth and Toller, with the *Concordance to Anglo-Saxon Poetry*, with the notes of Klaeber, Fry, and Dobbie, and my own hunches. My approach was contemplative. That is to say, I did not drive immediately toward an exact metaphrase (though I scribbled down a hurried first version as a sort of crude prototype of what would evolve), but hoped, through my researches of individual words and their appearances in different passages, through my repeated reading of each line, to hear the movement and the music of thought and feeling each line, or sentence, possessed. Both in the act of reading and interpreting and in the act of finding an equivalent expression of this reading in Modern English, I seemed to approach the final ideal version asymptotically, by successively more successful approximations. As I never consider my reading of any passage absolute and final, so do I never consider my translated version finished.

For instance, consider the first verse sentence of this passage (513–15a). Nothing in this is very problematic to the student of Old English. "Gewiton" here clearly corresponds in meaning to definition 2a in Bosworth and Toller: "to turn one's eyes with the intention of taking that direction, to set out towards, to start, pass over, depart," and so on, occurring "with the infinitive of a verb of motion."[39] The "wīgend" ("warriors"—whoever they may be— Danes or Frisians) set out homeward ("wīca nēosian"—literally, "to visit homes").[40] A very similar construction occurs at line 2162 of "Genesis"—"Gewat him þa se healdend ham siðian."[41] Grendel also goes home ("wīca nēosan") in line 125 with his slaughter spoils, as the Hetwar who encounter Beowulf do not ("lȳt eft becwōm / fram þām hildfrecan hāmes nīosan"). Thus, "wīca nēosian" is a collocation the poet is fond of, and it has the meaning of, roughly, "to go home." "Frēondum befeallen," quite unambiguously, means "deprived of friends"—it is a participial phrase modifying the "wīgend." "Frȳsland gesēon" is a verb phrase parallel to "wīca nēosian" and clearly means "to visit Frisia,"[42] though, problematically, that would seem to imply that Finnsburg is not in Frisia. "Hāmas ond hēaburh"[43] is a variation of "wīca" and translates as "homes and high (great?) town," though Klaeber counsels that "'hēaburh' is a high-sounding epic term that should not be pressed."[44] Thus, we have, in the most servile metaphrase, the approximation:

> Set out themselves the warriors to go home,
> deprived of friends to visit Frisia,
> home and high-town.

But Hengest had no such luck: he stayed or dwelled ("wunode") with Finn that "wælfāgne winter." The phrase "ðā gȳt" is one of those transparent collocations whose simplicity, at second glance, is at risk. Klaeber notes two uses in *Beowulf* (47 and 1050) where it means "further, besides."[45] Here it seems to mean rather "still, then." Hengest yet remained with Finn (at that time). The metrical emphasis falls heavily on "gȳt," as the sense demands. (Hengest, unlike the "wīgend," *yet* remained: he cannot see his home.) Instead, he remained with Finn that winter. Some irony, I believe, was intended by that contrast.

The winter was "wælfāgne," a problematic adjective. Bosworth and Toller conjecture "deadly hostile," interpreting "fah" as "hostile" and not "adorned," which it might mean.[46] "Wæl" itself may be interpreted in two ways: as "the slain" (from the root "walu") or "corpse" or "carnage."[47] Thus, as an element in compounds, it may mean "baleful, deadly, murderous, violent."[48] The *Beowulf* poet favors the use of "wæl" in this sense in compounds. I count twenty-two such compounds, several of which are used more than once. Thus, "wælfāgne" would mean "slaughter-stained"[49] or "blood-stained."[50]

However, among those numerous "wæl" compounds is one of a different breed, "wælrāpas," which occurs in line 1610 as part of a lovely simile describing the dissolution of the "þyrse"-envenomed blade: "hit eal gemealt īse gelicost, / þonne forstes bend Fæder onlæteð, / onwindeð wælrāpas" (1608–10a) ("it all melted most like ice, / when the Father loosens the bonds of frost, / unbraids the water-ropes"). Here, obviously, the meaning of "wæl" is "water."

And so "wælfāgne" might mean "water-hostile"; the image then is of violent winter seas that make all sailing perilous.

The translator has a choice. I opted for the former meaning since it makes harsher the bitterness of Hengest's enforced dwelling with Finn, the killer of Hnæf. The emphasis, quite reasonably, ought to be on the human violence that, to all those involved in the feud and especially to Hengest, has stained the winter with blood. The translation of "wælfāgne" as "slaughter-stained" is in keeping with a conception of the *Beowulf* poet as a master of Anglo-Saxon psychology.

Believing the poet is now concentrating on the tragic contradictions of Hengest's position in Finn's court, I chose the emendation "eal unhlitme" and the reading that interprets it as Dobbie does: "'without casting of lots'; that is, Hengest, having no choice, was forced to remain with Finn."[51]

It follows that Hengest might well have "eard gemunde"—"remembered home"—in such strait circumstances. (There is pathos now in the contrast with the more fortunate "wīgend" who spend the winter at home.) "Gemunde" is the third person singular of the past tense of "gemunian"—"to remember," to call to mind."[52]

My emendation, and reading, of the next line (1130) would also follow quite logically: Hengest would remember his home (and with what longing!) only if he could *not* drive (or pilot) on the sea his "hringedstefnan," his "ring-prowed ship."

The lines are closely wrought, built on the contrast between the warriors, who, though bereft of friends, are able to visit their homes—the variation, as well as the music of the lines, suggests

The Act of Translation

the freedom of the fortunate ones—and Hengest, who is compelled to stay.

Thus the metaphrase for the remaining lines of this passage:

> Hengest at that time yet
> slaughter-stained winter lived with Finn
> without choice; remembered his home,
> although he could not on the sea drive
> his ring-prowed thing.

In my first working, I simply attempted to get a readable trot, with no refinement:

> Then the warriors departed to go home,
> bereft of friends, to visit Frisia,
> their homes and high-estate. Hengest yet remained
> that slaughter-stained winter dwelling with Finn
> against his will; he remembered his native country
> though he could not pilot on the sea
> his ring-prowed ship.

At this stage, several phrases already seemed effective—"bereft of friends," "slaughter-stained winter," "ring-prowed ship." They seemed faithful, if not masterful, equivalents of the original words. I did not consider them cast in bronze, but they would do, at least for the time being.

Then I turned my attention to lines 1125a–27a. Hardest of my tasks there was to achieve a sound effect analogous to what seemed to me the music of release. Line 1125, in particular, is a long-vowelled line with a quick, unimpeded rhythm (the phrase wants to be read whole, and so the voice leaps quickly across the caesura): the rhythmic image, I believe, of the warriors' glad (despite "frēondum befeallen") return home. It suggested to me something of the explosive release of children from a schoolroom on a spring day. My second version did not satisfy me in this regard:

> The warriors departed homeward then,
> bereft of friends, saw their native Frisia,
> homes and gleaming halls.

I needed more movement: "Then the warriors set off homeward"? "Hastened"? Then I tried: "They hastened away, the warriors went home." Nearer the mark; the vowel music was analogous to the original, though the caesura in this version, enforced by the comma, is more emphatic than in the original.

I took liberties with the verb in the next line—"gesēon" means "perceive" or, in this instance, "visit," I believe: "bereft of friends, they dispersed into Frisia." The whole verb structure is "Gewiton . . . nēosian . . . gesēon." And that suggested the movement of "disperse." (I confess uneasiness with the word—its meaning is fine, but its sound will always suggest to me the movement of gases rather than men.) Though Klaeber counsels not to fret overmuch about "hēaburh," the word did cause me a minor headache. Clearly, "high town" or "high fort" (Chickering) would not do.[53] It is one of those grand words like "wuldortorhtan" (1136) that our poet, in an imperial mood, now and again permits himself. I sought something equally high-sounding, with an archaic and pretentious flavor, and hit upon—after many efforts (best forgotten)—"high demesne." "Demesne," as the *OED* notes, is a differentiated spelling of domain. I used it in the sense of "possession: an estate possessed" and, by extension, "the land or territory subject to a king or a prince"—as Keats used it in "On First Looking Into Chapman's Homer."[54] I do not, however, intend it to withstand fierce public scrutiny: the regal aura and Keatsian patina are enough.

That gave me, "They hastened away, the warriors went home, / bereft of friends, they dispersed in Frisia, / their halls and high demesne." It will be noted that "hāmas" became "halls" to avoid redundancy.

What I wanted most of all in this passage—beyond a fair approximation of the sense—was a rhythm equivalent to the original. Through rhythm, I believe, the poet makes palpable the contrast between the "wīgend's" release and Hengest's constriction. Hengest is bound to a prince he must despise; his enforced relationship with Finn is a parody of the natural relationship of lord and retainer. Instead of thinking how he can best serve Finn in return for munificent gifts, he must plot Finn's murder. And so, as Stanley noted, we have the image in lines 1131–33 of the storm-beaten sea and ice-locked channels acting as an objective correlative of Hengest's cold and savage mood.[55]

Tinkering some with the lines of my first working, I came up with: "their homes and high demesne. Hengest yet / stayed with Finn that slaughter-stained / winter against his will." By that short and hard half-line, "Hengest yet," I meant to contrast the hardness of Hengest's condition with that of the "wīgend," something the poet does in similar fashion at line 1127. The enjambment of my next line is a liberty and creates what might be called a syntactic pun—"winter against his will"—suggesting the winter itself is a force enlisted against Hengest. I am not pleased with the long-vowelled music of my version of line 1128, although, I might argue, it may suggest the length of Hengest's reluctant tenure.

"Eard gemunde" is a wonderful half-line: the laconic Anglo-Saxon style at its best. How much is there withheld! Obviously, I needed a terse equivalent, not the lengthy, "He beheld his homeland / in his mind's eye" of my second working, although I liked its music. "Homeland," for "eard," however, was right. "He longed for his homeland"? Not laconic enough: excessive sentiment. "He thought of his homeland"? Better. But why not suppress the implied "he"? And "remembered" is preferable to "thought of." Inadequate, but it must do. Alas, the translator cannot write the exact equivalent: "thought homeland."

With the emendation, the next line and a half (1130–31a) poses no major difficulties, beyond the usual necessary betrayals. "Hringedstefnan," which occupies all of 1131a, is a beautiful compound. It occurs only in *Beowulf*—here, and at lines 32 and 1897. "Hringed" means "formed of rings" or "of ring-like shape"; "stefn" means "stem" or "prow."[56] Thus Klaeber translates the compound as "ring-prowed ship,"[57] though, literally, of course, it means the "ring-prowed thing." Chickering, in his commentary on "hringedstefna" (32) writes that the image suggests a ship roughly like "the Oseberg ship. . . . This vessel has interlace carvings on its prow and stern whose stems each rise to a beautiful scroll."[58] I relied on the image of the Oseberg ship, studying the magnificent photographs in the Nordbok, *The Vikings:* the stem itself is coiled at its beak like a fiddlehead, suggesting the knot of energies at the lead shoot of a vigorous plant; the keel and plank lines of the ship sweep up, wavelike, and seem to unfurl at that point.[59] Even suspended in a museum room, the boat shape, with its coiling tendril of a prow, seems alive with movement. Perhaps the Anglo-Saxons were susceptible to the kinesthesia in the lines of the motionless ship, and so that feeling may have suggested such an adjective as "ūtfūs" (33)—"outward-eager." Such a ship must have always seemed ready for sea voyage.

For all that, I did not hit upon a compound that satisfied me more than Klaeber's suggestion, although I tried many ("scroll-prowed," "curving prowed," "coiling prowed," "coiling stemmed," and so on). So I translated these lines—"though he could not pilot his ring-prowed / ship on the sea." For this run of lines, my final translation was:

> They hastened away, the warriors went home,
> bereft of friends, they dispersed into Frisia,
> their halls and high demesne. Hengest yet
> stayed with Finn that slaughter-stained
> winter against his will, remembered his homeland,
> though he could not pilot his ring-prowed
> ship on the sea.

A swatch of lines such as these, by no means exceptional in their opacity, reveals one translator's handling of the hermeneutic motion. Each comma and semicolon, each emendation and proffered reading of a difficult word is a kind of freezing of the original text, a limitation of its manifold possibilities. This is true of any great text from an earlier, and other, civilization. Such texts are inexhaustible almost as nature and will continue to generate new translations, as new minds encounter them and as languages and cultures evolve new modes of seeing and saying. The Hindu god Krishna, I suspect, has had many avatars for much the same reason: no single incarnation can manifest all of his awesome energies, and each age requires an image that embodies him freshly in its own vocabulary, so to speak, restoring the god to his proper glory. A translation of *Beowulf*, though uncertain from line to line, a congeries of guesswork, speculation, and good luck, is a new incarnation of the poem, one of the myriad possible. The problem, if the reader will permit me to extend the metaphor a little further, is that the god's back is turned to us; the poem looks out on the Anglo-Saxon audience and their vanished memories. At times it may seem to the translator that he is working against its will and that the page of text is a blank wall.

3

Other passages, in substance at least, are not so opaque. I suggested briefly in my first chapter that *Beowulf* may find, at the close of the twentieth century, a translator with a special affinity for the poem's great theme of human mortality. Because the translator and his audience share the threat of nuclear holocaust, they face together an abyss not unlike the dark future drawn for the Geats by the messenger on the cliff. The contemporary translator is particularly attuned to hearing the music of loss, the elegiac strain, in *Beowulf*. Even when the reading of individual words is in question, the human meaning may be unmistakable, as in the last lines of the simile Beowulf draws between the grieving

Hrethel and the old man whose only son has been hanged (2455–61):

>   Gesyhð sorhcearig   on his suna būre
>   wīnsele wēstne,   windge reste
>   rēote berofene,   rīdend swefað,
>   hæleð in hoðman;   nis þær hearpan swēg,
>   gomen in geardum,   swylce þær iū wæron.
>   Gewiteð ponne on sealman,   sorhlēoð gæleð
>   ān æfter ānum;   þūhte him eall tō rūm,
>   wongas ond wīcstede.

I found this passage radiant. At such moments, the translator is borne along by the music and the meaning of the whole passage. He relies more on his own experience of loss and mortality than he does on the text. In such instances, when some commonality of shared humanity provides the translator with the key to a passage, I would endorse the freedom of imitation. Not that the translator should alter the central contours of the image—the old man facing his dead son's empty hall. But the translator ought to be at liberty to transform the accidental particulars of the imagery.

The translator must trust those moments when an affinity with the text permits a glimpse of what Walter Benjamin called "universal language": the archetype of which the poem itself is an incarnation.[60] This does not mean the translator can forego the initial hermeneutic motion; he must utilize all the sources of light available to him, including his researches into lexical and syntactic meaning by those means previously examined in this chapter. But if his intuitions tell him to overleap the metaphrase, he must. I have been critical of Burton Raffel's free and easy relationship with the text of *Beowulf* and the scholarly resources a translator must rely on, believing Raffel plays the role of the inspired bard-cum-translator with an overbreezy confidence. Indeed, the translator as well as Heremod may be guilty of *superbia*. But worse, perhaps, he may be craven and refuse the gift of the luminous moment and what arguably may be the sole justification for taking on the translation of a poem that has been translated so often, occasionally with some success.

According to the frequently used martial metaphor, the translator invades the poem and takes the meaning home captive, embodying the old content in the alien lexicon of the target language. The hermeneutic act is aggressive and violent and, unless something is given back to the poem, unethical.[61] Those luminous, those clairvoyant moments, I am suggesting, validate the whole uncertain enterprise of translation. The translator repetitions the source and completes the hermeneutic motion. He collaborates with the poet's old collaborator, one mortal's solitary communion with the Mysterium. In that moment, he is perhaps granted the translator's equivalent of the Visio: he approaches the silence that nourished the poet. The Mexican poet Octavio Paz writes, "The starting point of poetry, like that of religion, is the original human situation—being there, knowing we have been thrown into that *there* that is the hostile or indifferent world—and the fact that makes it precarious among all others: its temporality, its finitude."[62] It is at that moment, when the translator is most intensely aware of his solidarity with that which suffers time, that he may come close to the kind of knowing the *Beowulf* poet drew on when he coined that simile for Hrethel's grief.

I began my translation of this passage as I did every other. I puzzled over the possible interpretations of "rēote," "hoðman," and "sealman"—all very rare words with uncertain meanings. I savored the beautiful compound, "sorhlēoð" ("grief-song") and noted that the only other occurrence of the word was at line 67 of "The Dream of the Rood," where the mourners of the crucified Christ sing a "sorhlēoð."[63] I marvelled at the passionate restraint (how often is less more in *Beowulf!*) of "þūhte him eall tō rūm, / wongas ond wīcstede" ("thought them all too spacious, / the fields and dwellings"). Then I wrote a first draft that most scholars would consider a defensible reading of the passage:

> Grieving, he gazes on his son's dwelling,
> the empty wine-hall, the wind-swept resting place
> deprived of joy—the rider sleeps,
> the warrior in the grave; there is no harp music,
> joy in the courtyards, as there was before.
> He goes then to his couch, sings a grief-song,
> the one for the other; he thought them all too spacious,
> the fields and the dwellings.

Here indeed is the stuff of great poetry—so much is apparent even with the lines stripped of their music and the words muted and diminished in the callous act of metaphrase. But I did not work from this raw version so much as from the music of the original and my penetration, after contemplating the words, into the meaning. I knew that here I could relax for a moment my scholar's eye and depend on my training as a poet. The author had found an elemental form of human grief. A man or woman gazing on an object steeped in the presence of the absent beloved: this is the paradigm of all elegy and a movement of feeling that recurs again and again throughout *Beowulf*. I must go behind the words and allow other, collateral images to seep up from the original wellspring:

> In his grief he gazes on his son's house,
> the deserted hall, the draughty fire-place
> where the wind is chattering—the horseman sleeps,
> the soldier in his sepulchre; there is no stirring of
> harp or hawk as there was before.
> He turns then to his bed, the one alone
> sings a grief-song for the absent one—
> all too spacious the plains and the dwelling places.

No reading of the original text can give "the draughty fire-place / where the wind is chattering." Yet I do not consider my version faithless: the empty hall, with its smokehole above the stone hearth, might give such an impression to an old man haunting his son's familiar paths. The hall for the Anglo-Saxon was the archetypal node for human warmth and fellowship: "seledrēam" (2252)—"hall-joy"—is one of the poet's compounds. Consequently, there could be no greater image of human desolation for the Anglo-Saxon than the deserted hall. I seized on one feature of the hall—the cold hearth—as a sort of synecdoche for the whole. The image of the chattering wind, of course, is my own introduction; it seemed, however, true to the paradigm. Chattering suggests coldness ("chattering teeth"), a mortal fear, and the meaningless inhuman smalltalk of the elements, so dreadful when it invades a place famous for ceremonious human conversation.

Lines 2459–61a haunt me. There in brief is all that makes Anglo-Saxon poetry so great and so impervious to translation: the compression—"ān æfter ānum"; the understatement—þūhte eall tō rūm, / wongas ond wīcstede"; the exquisitely wrought compound—"sorhlēoð"; the word of uncertain provenance—"sealman." Has grief been conceived of elsewhere as a kind of agoraphobia, as if the surroundings had been so emptied of presence by the son's death that the father is suddenly conscious of the fearful spaciousness of things?

No modern translation can adequately register the compression of "ān æfter ānum"—"the one for the other." But the literal metaphrase misses the possible meaning of "ān" as the "only one" or the "one alone."[64] Nor does "other" or "other one" have the music of "ānum"—the vowel plus the "m" sound seems, for no logical reason, congruent to the mood of loss and deprived solitude. My version attempts to echo that music. Having stretched this line and a half out to two with my gloss of "ān" and "ānum," I suppressed, riskily, "þūhte him." My dash scarcely works in any logical fashion—rather it may suggest that the "grief-song" is a consequence of the perception that the fields are all too spacious and tie a loose ligature between the "absent one" and that perception. Lacking such a serviceable word as "rūm" ("roomy" will not do) to indicate the open emptiness of the house and the surrounding fields, I sought an appropriate vowel music—the linked, long "a" assonance of my line 2463.

I am groping here, trying to explain why my version is valid, despite the large liberties I took. I do not mean to reiterate the truism that the translator abides by the spirit rather than the letter, nor to suggest that he must always dive into the desolate mere to retrieve fresh images collateral to the poet's own. To any translator, the text of *Beowulf* is, by necessity, a chiaroscuro; in the general darkness there will be swards of light, runs of lines more easily accessible to his intelligence than others. Quite naturally, he will feel greater freedom—as if several links had been added to his chain—when he works with these lines. Instead of stumbling from phrase to phrase, his mind glides easily along an entire verse paragraph, and this easy movement is audible in the securer cadences of the translated poetry. The reader senses these lines were cast whole, not piecemeal and then stitched crudely together. In this passage and a number of others such grace, I believe, made my usual gravity more nimble.

This grace, if it may be called that, does not come at will. To translate nearly thirty-two hundred lines, the translator must set himself a routine and stick to it; he can only hope "the lively understandable spirit" visits more than seldom. In the intervals between such visitations he must cleave to the poem as closely as he can, utilizing the scholar's tools and the craftsman's formal intelligence. The breath, the anima, of his work comes from those brief visits; but the handsomeness of the work's body and bones stems from his more dependable acquirements.

The translator, then, would do well to view himself as a sober (though not abstemious) journeyman who has had the good luck to find employ on some large job of restoration—the facade, say, of a rainworn monumental pile. Time has done its work on the friezes over the west portal—they picture men in metal gear fighting on a narrow space before a cliff. But who are they? The journeyman may guess, but he cannot say for sure. And the heraldic animals on the stone capitals have been blotched and darkened by lichen; the coiled dragon's torso has been chipped and scaled by the ice storms of ten centuries. The same is true for the waterspout—that blurred and hunched grotesque under the building's eaves. The builder can barely descry its voluminous jaw, the pouch hanging from its naked haunch. The journeyman has his work cut out for him, but at least he does not work alone. The partners of his work are legion (find some of their names appended in the bibliography of this book). Indeed, one would think the scaffolding on which he works might fail to support such a large crew. Cheek by jowl, he works with them in all weathers for a year, two years—perhaps for a lifetime—and the facade keeps its gray ancient look, except that the lineaments of the heroic figures on the frieze seem slightly less blurred and the cliff face by which they struggle seems nearer. Only in his sleep, does he sometimes glimpse the cathedral restored, the stone fresh from the quarry, unweathered, flecked with mica, each sharp detail of sculpted hand and scaled wing, metal cloak and incisored mouth—the whole monument bathed in a hard wintry light.

Notes

Chapter 1. On the Translation of *Beowulf*

1. Vladimir Nabokov, "The Servile Path," in *On Translation,* ed. Reuben Brower (Cambridge: Harvard University Press, 1959), 97.
2. Werner Winter, "Impossibilities of Translation," in *The Craft and Context of Translation,* ed. William Arrowsmith and Roger Shattuck (Garden City, N.Y.: Anchor Books, 1964), 93.
3. *The Works of John Dryden,* ed. Edward Niles Hooker et al., (Berkeley: University of California Press, 1956), 1:114–15.
4. Ibid., 116.
5. Ibid., 117.
6. Ibid.
7. Ibid.
8. For an excellent study of the modern practice of translation and the strong influence exerted by Ezra Pound on contemporary translators, I would refer the reader to Ronnie Apter, *Digging for the Treasure: Translation after Pound* (New York: Peter Lang, 1984; reprint, New York: Paragon House Publishers, 1987).
9. "In the prefaces to the *Cura Pastoralis* and to the *Boethius,* Alfred, translating a well-known Latin tag, says his rendering is *hwilum word be worde, hwilum andgit of andgite.* Yet there is little word-for-word translation in these two works, or in the *Soliloquies* or in the *Orosius.*" Dorothy Whitelock, "The Prose of Alfred's Reign," in *Continuations and Beginnings,* ed. E. G. Stanley (London: Thomas Nelson, 1966), 79.
10. Walter Benjamin, "The Task of the Translator," trans. James Hynd and E. M. Valk, *Delos* 2 (1969): 88.
11. George Steiner, *After Babel* (New York: Oxford University Press, 1977), 296.
12. Ibid.
13. Ibid., 297–98.
14. Theodore Savory, *The Art of Translation* (London: Jonathan Cape, 1957), 40.
15. Steiner, *After Babel,* 298.
16. Ibid.
17. Ibid., 300.
18. Ibid., 301.
19. E. Talbot Donaldson, trans., *Beowulf* (New York: Norton, 1975), xiii.
20. Steiner, *After Babel,* 301.
21. John Leyerle, "The Interlace Structure of *Beowulf,*" *University of Toronto Quarterly* 37 (1967): 1–17.
22. Steiner, *After Babel,* 302.
23. Ibid., 452.
24. Ibid., 452–53.

25. Quoted in ibid., 267.

26. Jackson Mathews, "Third Thoughts on Translating Poetry," in *On Translation*, ed. Reuben Brower (Cambridge: Harvard University Press, 1959), 76.

27. Dorothy Whitelock, *The Audience of Beowulf* (Oxford: Clarendon Press, 1951), 36.

28. Ibid.

29. T. A. Shippey, *Beowulf* (London: Edward Arnold, 1978), 27.

30. Quoted by Charles Green, *Sutton Hoo* (London: Merlin Press, 1963), 70.

31. H. R. Ellis Davidson, *The Sword in Anglo-Saxon England* (Oxford: Clarendon Press, 1962). The translator finds himself assiduously ransacking every archaeological study he can lay his hands on. In a sense, little that has been published on the poem's cultural context will prove useless to him. The reader will find a selection of such studies consulted in the bibliography. Here I will only note a few of the most illuminating: Rupert Bruce-Mitford, *Aspects of Anglo-Saxon Archaeology* (London: Victor Gollancz, 1974); Rosemary Cramp, "Beowulf and Archaeology," *Medieval Archaeology* 1 (1957): 57–77; George Henderson, *Early Medieval* (Harmondsworth: Penguin Books, 1972); Knut Stjerna, *Essays on Questions Connected with the Old English Poem of Beowulf*, trans. John R. Clark Hall (London: Curtis and Beamish, 1912).

32. Rudolph Pannwitz, "The Shock of the Foreign," trans. W. S. Duell, *Delos* 4 (1970): 199.

33. Howell D. Chickering, trans., *Beowulf* (Garden City, N.Y.: Anchor Press/Doubleday, 1977), x–xi.

34. Kevin Crossley-Holland, trans., *Storm* (New York: Farrar, Straus, & Giroux, 1970), 31.

35. Ben Belitt, *Adam's Dream* (New York: Grove Press, 1978), 29.

36. J. R. R. Tolkien, Prefatory Remarks, *Beowulf*, trans. John Clark Hall (London: Allen & Unwin, 1967), ix.

Chapter 2. Choosing the Form

1. Donaldson, *Beowulf*, xiii.
2. Ibid., xvi.
3. David Wright, trans., *Beowulf* (Bungay: Richard Clay, 1957), 24.
4. Ibid., 24–25.
5. Ibid., 25.
6. Donaldson, *Beowulf*, 13.
7. Edwin Morgan, trans., *Beowulf* (Berkeley: University of California Press, 1964), xiv.
8. Quoted in ibid.
9. Ibid., xv; Raffel, trans., *Beowulf* (Amherst: University of Massachusetts Press, 1971), 93; Fr. Klaeber, ed., *Beowulf*, 3d ed. (Lexington, Mass.: D. C. Heath and Company, 1950), cxxxi.
10. William Ellery Leonard, trans., *Beowulf* (New York: Heritage Club, 1939), 1.
11. Leonard, *Beowulf*, vi.
12. Mary Waterhouse, trans., *Beowulf*, Preface (Cambridge: Bowes and Bowes, 1949).
13. Francis B. Gummere, "The Translation of *Beowulf*, and the Relations of Ancient and Modern English Verse," *American Journal of Philology* 7 (1886): 52–53.

14. Ibid., 53.
15. Ibid.
16. Morgan, *Beowulf,* xiii.
17. Ibid.
18. The vitality of this resurgence can be seen in the recent poetry anthology *Strong Measures: Contemporary American Poetry in Traditional Forms,* ed. Philip Dacey and David Jauss (New York: Harper and Row, 1986).
19. Robert Lowell, *Imitations* (New York: Farrar, Straus and Cudahy, 1961), xi–xii.
20. Waterhouse, *Beowulf,* 26.
21. Stanley Greenfield, "Esthetics and Meaning and the Translation of Old English Poetry," in *Old English Poetry,* ed. Daniel Calder (Berkeley: University of California Press, 1979), 101.
22. Ibid.
23. Morgan, *Beowulf,* xvi.
24. Greenfield, "Esthetics," 100.
25. Ibid.
26. Richard Eberhart, *Collected Poems* (New York: Oxford University Press, 1976), 105.
27. W. B. Yeats, *Essays and Introductions* (New York: Macmillan, 1973), 163.
28. Harvey Gross, *Sound and Form in Modern Poetry* (Ann Arbor: University of Michigan Press, 1973), 54.
29. T. S. Eliot, "Burnt Norton," in *The Complete Poems and Plays* (New York: Harcourt, Brace, & World, 1962), 118.
30. A. J. Bliss, "The Appreciation of Old English Metre," in *English and Medieval Studies,* ed. Norman Davis and Charles L. Wrenn (London: Unwin Brothers, 1962), 31–32.
31. Marjorie Daunt, "Old English Verse and English Speech Rhythm," in *Essential Articles for the Study of Old English,* ed. Jess B. Bessinger, Jr. and Stanley J. Kahrl (Hamden, Conn.: Archon Books, 1968), 300.
32. Theodore Roethke, "Some Remarks on Rhythm," in *On the Poet and His Craft,* ed. Ralph J. Mills, Jr. (Seattle: University of Washington Press, 1974), 74.
33. Henry C. Wyld, "Experiments in Translating *Beowulf,*" in *Studies in English Philology: A Miscellany in Honor of Frederick Klaeber,* ed. Kemp Malone and Martin Rudd (Minneapolis: University of Minnesota Press, 1929), 217.
34. Michael Alexander, trans., *Beowulf* (Harmondsworth: Penguin Books, 1973), 89.
35. Morgan, *Beowulf,* 33.
36. Bliss, "Appreciation," 29; Daunt, "Old English Verse," 290.
37. Thomas Cable, *The Meter and Melody of Beowulf* (London: University of Illinois Press, 1974), 11.
38. J. R. R. Tolkien, *Tree and Leaf; Smith of Wooton Major; and The Homecoming of Beorhtnoth Beorhthelm's Son* (London: Unwin Paperbacks, 1975), 161.
39. Daunt, "Old English Verse," 290.

Chapter 3. Diction

1. Wyld, "Experiments," 218–19.
2. Geoffrey Leech, *A Linguistic Guide to English Poetry* (London: Longmans, Green, 1969), 13.
3. Thomas Gray, *The Correspondence of Thomas Gray,* ed. Paget Toynbee and Leonard Whibley (Oxford: Clarendon Press, 1935), 1:192.

4. Both Leech and Bateson have commented on this phenomenon: "Much of the old paraphernalia of poetic expression (e.g. archaism) has been overthrown, and poets have eagerly delved into the most unlikely resources, such as the terminology of aeronautics and finance. . . . In the new poetry of the fifties, this flamboyance has given way to a more sober and easy acceptance of colloquialism, even slang, as a fit medium of poetic expression," Leech, *Linguistic Guide*, 23. "A poetry that is coextensive with the language in which it is written has always been extremely rare. Dryden was the last English poet whose verse has even approached such a condition. But we are on the verge of such a poetry at this moment. The signs and portents are all around us," F. W. Bateson, *English Poetry and the English Language* (Oxford: Clarendon Press, 1973), 91.

5. Bateson, *English Poetry*, 91.

6. "Its [Old English poetry's] terms of expression were nuclei of meaning, symbols of integrated experience, aggregates of traditional associations rather than words delimited intellectually, as is most of our present-day vocabulary—a difference which is readily realized if we try to select a Modern English equivalent to such a conceptual term as Old English *dom* with its implications of judgment, free choice, authority, glory and renown: by using any single modern word we empty the Old English one of some of its meaning," Peter Clemoes, *Rhythm and Cosmic Order in Old English Christian Literature* (Cambridge: Cambridge University Press, 1970), 6.

7. Quoted by Randall Jarrell in *William Carlos Williams, Selected Poetry*, ed. Jarrell (New York: New Directions, 1949), xiv.

8. James M. Garnett, trans., *Beowulf* (Boston: Ginn, 1895), 19.

9. Charles Kennedy, trans., *Beowulf* (New York: Oxford University Press, 1940), 18.

10. Morgan, *Beowulf*, xi.

11. W. B. Yeats, "Meditations in Time of Civil War, III, My Table," in *The Collected Poems of W. B. Yeats* (New York: Macmillan, 1969), 200.

12. Tolkien, Prefatory Remarks, xviii–xix.

13. Tolkien, "The Homecoming," 166.

14. Morgan, *Beowulf*, 13.

15. "Instigated," *The Compact Edition of the Oxford English Dictionary* (New York: Oxford University Press, 1974).

16. Morgan, *Beowulf*, 20.

17. Steiner, *After Babel*, 327.

18. Ibid., 324.

19. Ibid., 339.

20. Donald Davie, *Purity of Diction in English Verse* (London: Chatto and Windus, 1952), 10–11.

21. Gavin Bone, *Anglo-Saxon Poetry* (Oxford: Clarendon Press, 1943), 11–12.

22. Arthur Brodeur, *The Art of Beowulf* (Berkeley: University of California Press, 1959), 8.

23. Ibid., 28.

24. Ibid., 18.

25. Ibid., 18–19.

26. Caroline Brady, "The Old English Nominal Compounds In '-rad,'" *PMLA* 67 (1952): 556.

27. Ibid., 568.

28. Brodeur, *Art of Beowulf*, 23–24.

29. Morgan, *Beowulf*, 9.

30. Raffel, *Beowulf*, 11.

31. Tolkien, Prefatory Remarks, xxiii.
32. Chickering, *Beowulf,* 67.
33. Alexander, *Beowulf,* 61.

Chapter 4. The Syntax of Contemplation

1. Brodeur, *Art of Beowulf,* 40.
2. Klaeber, *Beowulf,* lxv.
3. Brodeur, *Art of Beowulf,* 40.
4. Ibid., 39.
5. Leyerle, "The Interlace Structure of Beowulf," 4.
6. Ibid., 6.
7. Chickering, *Beowulf,* x.
8. Ibid., 191.
9. Donaldson, *Beowulf,* 41.
10. Kevin Crossley-Holland, trans., *Beowulf* (Cambridge: D. S. Brewer, 1977), 96.
11. Leyerle, "Interlace Structure," 2–4.
12. G. M. Hopkins, "I wake and feel the fell of dark, not day," 9–11, in *Poems and Prose of Gerard Manley Hopkins,* ed. W. H. Gardner (Harmondsworth: Penguin, 1975), 62.
13. Adeline Bartlett, *The Larger Rhetorical Patterns in Anglo-Saxon Poetry* (New York: Columbia University Press, 1935).
14. Thomas Hart, "*Ellen:* Some Tectonic Relationships in *Beowulf* and Their Formal Resemblance to Anglo-Saxon Art," *Papers on Language and Literature* 6 (1970), 263–90.
15. Tolkien, "The Monsters and the Critics," in *The Beowulf Poet,* ed. Donald Fry (Englewood Cliffs, N.J.: Prentice-Hall, 1968), 34.
16. Ibid., 36.
17. Ibid., 37.
18. Frederick Bracher, "Understatement in Old English Poetry," *PMLA* 52 (1937): 920.
19. Leech, *Linguistic Guide,* 170.
20. The reader is referred to 11. 11–14 of "The Wanderer," one of many passages in Old English poetry expressing a similar sentiment: ". . . and I know it for a truth / That in a man it is a noble virtue / To hide his thoughts, lock up his private feelings, / However he may feel," "The Wanderer," trans. Richard Hamer, in *A Choice of Anglo-Saxon Verse* (London: Faber and Faber, 1970), 175.
21. "A man should wait, before he makes a vow, / Until in pride he truly can assess / How, when a crisis comes, he will re-act," 70–72, "The Wanderer," trans. Richard Hamer, 179.
22. Henry C. Wyld, "Diction and Imagery in Anglo-Saxon Poetry," in *Essays and Studies by Members of the English Association* 11 (1925): 49–91.
23. I offer here only a sampling of the most significant scholarship: Brodeur, *Art of Beowulf,* 88–95; Greenfield, "Grendel's Approach to Heorot: Syntax and Poetry," in *Old English Poetry,* ed. Robert Creed (Providence: Brown University Press, 1967), 275–84; Alan Renoir, "Point of View and Design for Terror in *Beowulf,*" *Neuphilologische Mitteilungen* 63 (1962): 154–67.
24. Again, a sampling from that great hedge surrounding the mere: Charles Frey, "Lyric in Epic: Hrothgar's Depiction of the Haunted Mere," *English Studies* 58 (1977): 296–303; Alan Renoir, "The Terror of Dark Waters: A Note on

Virgilian and Beowulfian Techniques," in *The Learned and the Lewed*, ed. Larry Benson (Cambridge: Harvard University Press, 1974), 147–60; D. W. Robertson, Jr., "The Doctrine of Charity in Medieval Literary Gardens," *Speculum* 26 (1951): 24–49.

25. Walter Morris Hart, *Ballad and Epic, Studies and Notes in Philosophy and Literature* (Boston: Ginn & Company for Harvard University, 1907), 11:152.

26. Bartlett, *Rhetorical Patterns*, 7.

27. Brodeur, *Art of Beowulf*, 19–20.

28. Ananda Coomaraswamy, *Christian and Oriental Philosophy of Art* (New York: Dover Publications, 1956), 37.

29. Raffel, *Beowulf*, 38.

30. Morgan, *Beowulf*, 37.

31. Raffel, *Beowulf*, Afterword, 86.

32. Ibid.

33. Margaret Pepperdene, "Beowulf and the Coastguard," *English Studies* 47 (1966): 409–19.

34. Raffel, *Beowulf*, 16.

35. Chickering, *Beowulf*, 17.

36. I refer the reader to the previously cited articles by Leyerle and Hart as well as to Robert Burlin, "Inner Weather and Interlace," in *Old English Studies in Honour of John C. Pope*, ed. Robert Burlin and Edward Irving, Jr. (Toronto: University of Toronto Press, 1974), 81–89; Eamon Carrigan, "Structure and Thematic Development in *Beowulf*," *Proceedings of the Royal Irish Academy* 66 (1967): 1–51.

37. Joan Blomfield, "The Style and Structure of *Beowulf*," *Review of English Studies* 14 (1938): 397.

38. Klaeber, *Beowulf*, xxx.

39. Ibid., xxix–xxx.

40. Leyerle, "Interlace Structure," 8.

41. Ibid., 13.

42. Tolkien, "The Monsters," 22.

Chapter 5. The Act of Translation

1. Klaeber, *Beowulf*, 149.

2. Norman Eliason, "The Ðyle and Scop in *Beowulf*," *Speculum* 38 (1963): 269.

3. Adelaide Hardy, "The Christian Hero Beowulf and Unferð Ðyle," *Neophilologus* 53 (1969): 55–69.

4. Joseph L. Baird, "Unferth the Ðyle," *Medium Ævum* 39 (1970): 1–12.

5. Carol J. Clover, "The Germanic Context of the Unferth Episode," *Speculum* 55 (1980): 444–68.

6. *An Anglo-Saxon Dictionary*, by J. Bosworth and T. N. Toller (1882–98), s.v. "winnan."

7. Ibid., s.v. "sæ."

8. Ibid., s.v. "sund."

9. Ibid., s.v. "sund."

10. Ibid., s.v. "flitan."

11. *A Concordance to the Anglo-Saxon Poetic Records*, ed. J. B. Bessinger (1978), s.v. "flitan."

12. *An Anglo-Saxon Dictionary*, s.v. "wlenco."

13. *A Concordance*, s.v. "dol."

14. *An Anglo-Saxon Dictionary,* s.v. "dol."
15. Ibid., s.v. "gilp."
16. *A Concordance,* s.v. "lēof."
17. Ibid., s.v. "belēan."
18. Wrenn, *Beowulf,* 195.
19. *A Concise Anglo-Saxon Dictionary,* by John R. Clark Hall, 4th ed., s.v. "sīð."
20. *An Icelandic-English Dictionary,* by Richard Cleasby, et al., 2nd ed., s.v. "Ægir."
21. *An Anglo-Saxon Dictionary,* s.v. "strēam."
22. Ibid., s.v. "þeccean."
23. Ibid., s.v. "metan."
24. *A Concordance,* s.v. "merestrǣt."
25. Klaeber, *Beowulf,* s.v. "merestrǣt."
26. *An Anglo-Saxon Dictionary,* s.v. "bregdan."
27. Ibid., s.v. "glidan."
28. Ibid., s.v. "gārsecg."
29. R. L. M. Derolez, "'—And That Difficult Word, Garsecg' (Gummere)," *Modern Language Quarterly* 7 (1946): 445–52.
30. R. A. Williams, *The Finn Episode in Beowulf* (Cambridge: University Press, 1924), 2.
31. Dobbie, ed., *Beowulf and Judith,* 35–36.
32. Ibid., 177.
33. Donald K. Fry, ed., *Finnsburh Fragment and Episode* (London: Methuen and Co. Ltd., 1974), 43.
34. Chickering, *Beowulf,* 177.
35. Dobbie, ed., *Beowulf and Judith,* 36.
36. Fry, *Finnsburh Fragment,* 20–21.
37. Ibid., 43.
38. Cf. Klaeber, *Beowulf,* 43; Dobbie, *Beowulf and Judith,* 35; and Chickering, *Beowulf,* 112–14. Roy Leslie views Fry's editing here as mistaken on stylistic grounds and demonstrates why in "The Editing of Old English Poetic Texts: Questions of Style," in *Old English Poetry,* ed. Daniel Calder (Berkeley: University of California Press, 1979), 118–19.
39. *An Anglo-Saxon Dictionary,* s.v. "gewitan."
40. Ibid., s.v. "nēosan."
41. *A Concordance,* s.v. "gewat."
42. *An Anglo-Saxon Dictionary,* s.v. "gesēon."
43. Ibid., s.v. "hēaburh."
44. Klaeber, *Beowulf,* 174.
45. Klaeber, s.v. "gȳt."
46. *An Anglo-Saxon Dictionary,* s.v. "wælfāg."
47. Ibid., s.v. "wæl."
48. *A Short Dictionary of Anglo-Saxon Poetry,* by J. B. Bessinger, 1960 ed., s.v. "wæl—."
49. Klaeber, s.v. "wæl-fag."
50. Fry, s.v. "wælfāg."
51. Dobbie, *Beowulf and Judith,* 177.
52. *An Anglo-Saxon Dictionary,* s.v. "gemunian."
53. Chickering, *Beowulf,* 113.
54. *Oxford English Dictionary,* s.v. "demesne."
55. E. G. Stanley, "Old English Poetic Diction and the Interpretation of 'The Wanderer,' 'The Seafarer' and 'The Penitent's Prayer,'" *Anglia* 73 (1956): 439.

56. *An Anglo-Saxon Dictionary,* s.v. "hringed."
57. Klaeber, *Beowulf,* s.v. "hringed–stefna."
58. Chickering, *Beowulf,* 292.
59. Bertil Almgren et al., *The Viking* (Gothenberg: Nordbok, 1976), 257.
60. Benjamin, "Task of the Translator," 96.
61. Steiner, *After Babel,* 300.
62. Octavio Paz, *The Bow and the Lyre,* trans. Ruth L. C. Simms (Austin: University of Texas Press, 1973; reprint, New York: McGraw-Hill, 1975), 131 (page reference is to reprint edition).
63. *A Concordance,* s.v. "sorhlēoð."
64. *An Anglo-Saxon Dictionary,* s.v. "ān."

Part 2
A Translation of *Beowulf*

Beowulf

Listen!
We have heard of the Spear-Danes in earlier days,
of a lineage of kings who accomplished high deeds,
how the noble ones excelled in valor!
   Time and again, Scyld Scefing dispossessed
ravening bands of their mead-benches,   5
spread terror among men—he who, at first,
was a mere foundling: for that he had recompense,
he grew strong under the heavens, prospered in honors
until his power reached to outlying princes
beyond the whale's domain: they must kneel to him,   10
yielding tribute. That was a good king!
An heir was later born to him,
a child in the courtyards whom God had sent
to comfort that folk; He knew how pain
had cumbered them, leaderless   15
a long while; him, the Lord of Life,
Wielder of Glory, granted earthly gifts.
Beow won fame—his renown reached far—
Scyld's son in the northern lands.
So a young man must accomplish good   20
with fair gifts in his father's house
so that retainers will stand by him
in his great age, his people obey him
when war comes. By such praiseworthy deeds
men will prosper among all peoples.   25
   Scyld set out on the day ordained,
in his vigor went into the Lord's keeping.
They carried him to the verge of the sea,
his own retainers, as he himself had asked
when by such words he ruled the Scyldings: 30
the beloved land-founder had ruled long.
There at harbor swung the ring-carved prow,
the prince's voyager, icy, death-eager.
They laid him down, their dear lord,
the ring-giver in the lap of the ship,   35

that majesty by the mast. Treasures from afar
were heaped beside him, gold-adorned heirlooms;
never was a ship more generously outfitted
with war-gear and battle dress,
40   chain mail and falchion; on his chest lay
many treasures which must venture with him
far into the flood's dominion.
They furnished him with no fewer gifts—
ancestral heirlooms—than they provided
45   who sent him forth at the first shaping
a small boy, orphaned on the waves.
They set by him a golden standard,
high over his head, then let the sea take him,
gave him back to the breakers. Their spirits were grieving,
50   their minds cast down. Men did not know,
to say the truth, even hall counselors,
wise men under the heavens, who lay hold of that cargo.

    Then Beow of the Scyldings, beloved sovereign,
famed among his folk, held the strongholds
55   for a long while—his father passed on,
old from the earth—and to him in turn
the noble Healfdene was born; aged, war-hardened,
he ruled the Scyldings with a capable hand.
To him four children were counted in all,
60   born into this world, prudent men of action,
Heorogar and Hrothgar and Halga the good,
I have heard that . . . was Onela's queen,
bed companion of the Battle-Scylfing.
    Good luck at war was granted Hrothgar.
65   The brilliance of his victories made his men
proud to serve him, until they were tempered by age
and became a famous band. It came into his thought
he would command a building be made,
a great mead-hall erected by men
70   that after-comers should ever praise it,
and there within grant each a share,
both young and old alike, of God's largesse to him,
except common lands and the lives of men.
Then proclamation was made to many tribes
75   throughout Middle-Earth that the work begin,
the timbers be hewn. Quickly they set about
measuring and planing beams. In time, it was finished,

that greatest of halls. He shaped its name, "Heorot,"
that king who ruled wide by virtue of his words.
He did not renege: he gave fine rings, 80
white silver at the feasts. High and horn-gabled,
the hall rose up. Soon it would taste
the treachery of fire. Nor was it long
before knives unsheathed and hatred flared
after hot words between sworn kin. 85
   Then the bold demon who went by darkness
listened against his will and was steeped in pain
each day he heard the revel of men
ring out in the hall; there was harp music,
the clear voice of the poet. He who well remembered 90
told of the shaping of men long ago,
he said how the Almighty labored over the earth,
made the lovely plains, braiding them about with water,
he set as a victory sign the sun and moon,
twin lights for the land-dwellers, 95
and adorned each naked ridge and gap
with leaves and branches. Life also He shaped,
each of the species that swim or crawl.
So that company of men lived in a circle
of light and song, until one began, 100
a fiend in hell, to work evil.
The cruel spirit was named Grendel,
great edge-keeper, who held the moor,
the fen and fastness. The spawn of the tideland
was his for a time, the miserable creature's, 105
after the Shaper had branded them
as kinsmen of Cain—He avenged that killing,
the slayer of Abel knew God's ire—
he did not exult in that evil, but the Lord drove him out
from all fellowship for that fratricide. 110
From him, the unnatural awoke in nature,
giants and elves and the flesh-eating dead,
such titans that contended with God
through long ages; He gave them fair requital.

   When night had fallen, he crept nearer 115
the noble house to observe the Ring-Danes
and the guard they kept, after banqueting.
He found therein a company of aethelings,
asleep after feasting; they knew little grief,

120 sad birthright of men. That fell thing,
     grim and greedy, blood-ravenous,
     wasted no time. He seized from rest
     thirty men; then turned again
     for the door, gloating in his blood-gluttony,
125 to trudge home with his bundle of marrow bones.
     At daybreak, Grendel's battle-craft
     was brought to light, made known to men;
     after the feast, many wept,
     a loud dawn-lament. That great lord,
130 prince excelling all others, was sunk in grief,
     he suffered immeasurably the loss of his friends
     once they had found the blood-filled footprints
     of the cursed demon. Pain overpowered him,
     too fierce, too enduring. Nor did he wait
135 a single night to call again,
     more murderous than before, and did not mourn
     that slaughter and sin, the recalcitrant creature.
     Then it was easy to find those who preferred
     to take their rest at some distance,
140 sleep outside the stronghold, when the hall-keeper's hatred
     by such clear tokens, and true accounts,
     was broadcast to all. They saved their skins
     by staying away, those who fled the demon.
     So by blood he ruled, and warred against what is right,
145 alone against them all, until the fairest of halls
     stood desolate. That time was long:
     for twelve winters, the lord of the Scyldings
     endured every duress, deeply suffered
     enormous pain; in time it became
150 common knowledge among foreign men,
     lamented in song that Grendel fought
     a long time with Hrothgar, carried on that vendetta,
     that slaughter and sin, for many years,
     strife unceasing; nor would he sue for peace
155 from any man of the Danish tribe,
     pull in his talons, defray the death cost.
     No man of counsel had cause to foresee
     sweet balm from those bloody hands;
     but the death-shadow made them his prey,
160 youth and veteran he snared alike,
     hovering in ambush. By perpetual night

he held the shrouded moors. Men cannot know
whither glide such hell-seers.
    So, many evils, the foe of man—
the cruel outcast—often conceived,   165
humbling them: he possessed Heorot,
that jewel-bright hall, by swarthy night—
but he could not approach the gift-throne,
that treasure, because of God, nor know His thought.
That was great anguish to the friend of the Scyldings,   170
and broke his spirit. Many often sat
whispering in council; they sought a cure—
what fierce resolve might best accomplish
against that one who waited in his web.
Sometimes they sacrificed at heathen shrines,   175
kneeled to idols, calling them forth,
that the slayer of souls might intervene
in their time of need. Such was their custom,
vain hope of heathens; they honored hell
in mind and heart, but God they knew not,   180
the deeds of the Judge, what was due their Lord,
and how to praise Him, the Shield of Heaven,
Helmsman of the World. Woe unto them
who thrust their souls into the harness of fire
when afflicted: they can expect no consolation   185
for all is changeless there. All praise unto them
who after their death-day seek out their Lord,
and find repose in the breast of the Father.

    So the son of Healfdene constantly brooded
on that heavy loss; nor could the prudent man   190
turn away that woe: it was too vast,
cruel and persistent, which had befallen his folk,
violent duress, greatest of night-plagues.
    Rumors of Grendel's deeds reached Higelac's thane,
great among the Geats, in his homeland.   195
In his strength he dwarfed all other men
alive on the Earth in those days,
and was great-spirited. He commanded a ship
be rigged for travel, said he would seek
the war king over swan-tracked waves,   200
that great lord who had want of men.
Wise counselors did not dissuade him

from the expedition, though they held him dear:
they urged him on, studying the portents.
205 That great one of the Geat tribe
chose swordsmen of the keenest temper
he might obtain; one of fifteen,
he sought his ship, learned in sea-things,
he led the way to land's end.
210 Time hastened, the ship rode the waves,
the boat beneath sea-cliffs. Men in their eagerness
stepped over the gunnels; the surf was heavy,
thundered against the sand. They stowed
bright heirlooms, gold-adorned war-gear
215 in the ship's hold, then shoved out,
those men on the wished-for journey, their trim ship.
It sped over waves under a strong wind,
that foam-throated ship so like a sea-bird,
until soon after dawn on the second day
220 land was sighted and sailors could gaze
by the curving bowsprit on a stretch of beach
backed by glittering cliffs, a steep shore-range
and broad promontories. So the sea was crossed,
the voyage at end. Those men of the Weders
225 stepped quickly ashore, secured
their ship. Their metal shirts, war-cloaks
jinked brightly. They thanked God
that the crossing had been so easy.
    Then the Scylding guard gazed out from the wall,
230 he who must patrol the sea-beaten cliffs
saw bright shields, cunning war-gear
borne over the gang-plank; he was feverish
with desire to know who the men were.
Spurring his horse, he rode down to the shore,
235 Hrothgar's man, brandishing a spear
fiercely in his hand, and spoke these formal words:
"Who are you, in your steel harness,
your coats of mail, that have dared steer
your tall ship over the sea-ways,
240 hither on uncertain currents. Listen well:
I've kept sea-watch for a long time now,
making sure no raiders come ashore
to pillage and plunder the Danish land.
None have beached their ships more brazenly

than you men-at-arms and yet you await 245
no word of leave from our warriors,
consent from my kinsmen. Never have I seen
a greater man than that one there,
a champion in war-gear: nor is he someone's servant,
possessed of such weapons, unless his face belies him, 250
that singular visage. Now I must know
your lineage before you take another step—
spies that you may be—onto Danish soil.
You seafarers, strangers from afar,
hear now my naked thought: 255
you'd best make known straightway
whence you are come."

   The one in command, leader of that company,
measured his words carefully and well:
"We are all of us men of the Geats 260
and hearth-comrades of Higelac.
My father was well known among our folk,
a man of courage and courtesy called Ecgtheow;
he lived a long while before he left us,
praised by us all. Not a wise man 265
over all this earth but remembers him clearly.
Through a similar devotion we have come seeking
your own lord, the son of Healfdene,
shielder of a people. Counsel us well;
our mission to the glorious one, the lord 270
of the Danes, is of greatest import. I will not make
a mystery of it. You know very well,
if things stand as we've been led to believe,
that a vicious creature haunts the Scyldings,
a being feverish with hate who reveals himself 275
by acts of terror, unspeakable atrocities
committed in darkness. I may, through largesse
of spirit, give Hrothgar good counsel,
how that excellent old man might overthrow the enemy,
if any change is to come at all, 280
remedy for the bitter working of his affliction,
and those waves of pain recede some, and cool;
else, he will be grief's thrall always,
and that wound fester as long as it shines there,
that best of halls on its high hill." 285
   The guard spoke, the fearless sergeant

seated on his horse: "A veteran of war—
any man of sound judgment—must carefully sift
word and deed, and know the difference.
290 I glean this meaning from your speech: you are loyal
to the Scylding lord. Go forth, bearing
both weapon and war-cloak: I shall lead you.
I shall also command my troop of men
to keep your ship—this freshly caulked
295 craft on the sand—safe from every peril,
carefully attended, until it can bear
these dear men so ambitious of good
homeward to Wedermark over windy seas,
that curve-necked keel—those whom it is granted
300 to pass unscathed through the coming slaughter."
    They turned to go—the ship awaited them,
motionless on its moorings, the vessel with its empty hold
fast at anchor. Boar images shone
over cheek-guards blazoned with gold,
305 blood-marked and fire-hardened: the war-tempered helmets
guarded their lives. The men hurried on,
marching in file until they could see
the gold-shimmering ridgepole of Heorot,
most famous among earthdwellers
310 of the halls under heaven, in which the king waited.
It shone as a beacon over many lands.
That veteran hardened in battle
pointed out the bright hall, so they might go
directly there; then the warrior wheeled
315 his horse, and spoke these words:
"It is time I go. May the Almighty Father
keep you in His grace, sound and well
beneath His sceptre. I'm bound to the shore
to hold sea-watch for hostile raiders."

320   The street was paved, a mosaic of stone
easy to follow. Their chain mail shone,
each brilliant ring of hand-linked iron
sang in its harness, when they first came,
beautiful in death-gear, to the great hall.
325 The sea-travellers set broad shields
rimmed with metal against the wall.
Then they sat down: ringed mail clinked,
the men's war-shirts. Their spears, a holt

of naked ash, barbed grey at the tip,
stood by the sea-men. The iron-troop 330
was exalted with weapons.
                    Then a proud warrior
addressed those men-at-arms:
"Where is your homeland, you with emblazoned shields,
your grey armor, visored helms,
and all those spears? I am Hrothgar's 335
bodyguard, yet have not seen
so many foreign men of equal splendor.
I judge you have not come in exile and want,
but have sought Hrothgar from greatness of heart."
The one famed for courage answered him, 340
that proud man of the Geats, stern in his helmet,
spoke these words: "We are Higelac's
loyal kinsmen: Beowulf is my name.
I will tell your great lord and elder,
the son of Healfdene, my errand 345
if he will grant us leave
that we may appraoch his royal person."
Wulfgar spoke—a prince of the Vendels
whose firmness of mind was known to many,
his valor and wisdom: "I will consult 350
the friend and lord of the Scyldings,
this great king and dispenser of gifts,
about your mission as you request,
and swiftly bring you the answer
which the great one deems to give me." 355
   He went at once to where Hrothgar sat,
old and white-haired among his liege-men,
strode fearless until he stood before
the Danish lord as custom demanded.
Wulfgar spoke to his beloved king: 360
"The newcomers are a band of Geats,
arrived from afar over the sea's expanse.
These warriors call their leader
Beowulf. They courteously request
that they, my Lord, might exchange 365
words with you. However you answer,
do not refuse them, benevolent Hrothgar!
They, in their war-gear, would seem worthy
of greatest esteem. Indeed, the prince
who commands such followers is a capable man." 370

Hrothgar spoke, protector of the Scyldings:
"I knew him when he was a mere boy;
his father was called Ecgtheow.
Hrethel of the Geats gave him in marriage
375 his only daughter: it is his heir
who has come in his courage to visit his old ally.
Sailors who carry tribute, splendid
gifts to the Geats, have spoken of him:
they say this war-tempered one
380 has the strength of thirty men
in his hand-grip. Him holy God
sent us, the West Danes, a gift
of pure grace for the terror of Grendel:
that is my devout belief. I shall reward
385 his keenness of spirit with torques of gold.
Go quickly now, bid them to come,
this band of kinsmen assembled together.
And say also these words: they are welcome
among the Danes." Wulfgar went to the door
390 and announced to those gathered inside:
"I have been ordered by my liege lord,
King of the East Danes, to say he
recognizes your quality, that you are welcome,
whence you are come over the whelming flood.
395 Now you may go in your panoply of war,
your vizored helms, to your audience with Hrothgar;
but leave your shields and wooden shafts
tipped for killing to await you at the threshold."
    The great one stood up, encircled by his men,
400 that proud escort; some remained
to guard the battle-gear, as he sternly bade them.
The rest went at once—a guide was at hand—
into Heorot. Stern beneath his helmet,
the warrior positioned himself by the hearth.
405 Beowulf spoke—his chain mail shone,
a hard net sewn out of cunning fires:
"Health, Hrothgar, be yours! I am Higelac's
kinsman and retainer. I have sought glory
even in my youth. It happened that I heard
410 of this Grendel creature in my home country.
Seafarers say that this very hall,
fair though it be, stands tenantless,
abandoned by men after evening light,

heaven's radiance, fades from the sky.
Wise counselors, the most prescient 415
of all my people, persuaded me
to come to your aid—because, my lord Hrothgar,
they know the strength harbored in these hands.
They witnessed with their own eyes the bloody
gear I brought home when I wasted five 420
of the giant's brood, and on the waves slew
night-goers. I suffered duress
and took revenge—their just dessert—
squeezed the life from them; and now with Grendel,
the lawless demon, shall I alone 425
arrange a meeting. Lord of the Bright-Danes,
protector of the Scyldings, I will await
your dispensation, patient you will not
refuse my suit, guard of warriors,
benevolent prince, now I have come 430
so far: I, and my company of men,
this hardened band, will cleanse Heorot.
I have also heard the monster
is not shrewd enough to care about weapons.
Therefore, I scorn their use completely— 435
so Higelac will be blithe of spirit
I will bear neither sword nor metal-
enforced shield to combat—but will grapple hand-
to-hand with that devil and strive for life,
coupled beastlike with him. Then must the loser, 440
yielding to death, trust in God.
I am sure if he gets the upper hand
in that encounter he will eat his fill
of Geats, feed on Hrethel's kinsmen
as he has on yours. You will not have need 445
to close these staring eyes, but he will
hide me himself in his bloody gorge:
he will carry off my corpse, and plan a banquet,
mark the way with my blood, and himself be
sole guest and reveler. You'll not have need 450
to bother about the care of my corpse.
Send Higelac, if war takes me,
this fine coat of mail, best of garments,
guarding my breast. It was Hrethel's once,
the work of Weland. Let wyrd go as it must!" 455

Hrothgar spoke, protector of the Scyldings:
"Because of remembered deeds, as well as native virtue,
have you sought us, my dear Beowulf.
Your father stirred up the greatest of feuds:
460 he struck down Heatholaf of the Wylfings
in close combat; fearing reprisal,
the Weders dare not grant him asylum.
Therefore, he sought the South-Danes,
the proud Scyldings, over rough seas.
465 I had just come to the Danish throne
and in my youth held a large kingdom
and vast wealth. Heorogar,
my eldest brother, son of Healfdene,
had just died. He was better than I!
470 I settled the feud as swiftly as I could,
sent old treasures over mountainous waves
to the Wylfings. Your father swore me allegiance.
It is a bitter thing for me to confess
what humiliations and helpless loss
475 Grendel's hatred, his instinctual malice,
has brought home to me. My hall troop
is waned to a handful. Wyrd has swept them away
into Grendel's claw. If God would only sever
the vicious thing from its deeds!
480 Time and again, drunk with beer,
deep in their cups, men have boasted
how they would deal with Grendel
here in this hall with their fearsome swords.
Sunrise would bring to light
485 a different story: the gore-spattered
hall, bench planks dripping with blood,
and blood everywhere! Then I had a few less
of my dear ones whom death had carried off.
Sit now to eat and be at your ease,
490 speak, as your mind urges, of human triumphs."
    Room was made for all the Geats,
benches cleared in the mead-hall.
Swiftly the young men, proud in their strength,
took their places. Observing the old usage,
495 one bore a hammered cup in his hand
and poured the shimmering drink. A scop sang
bright song in Heorot. There was the pleasure of men,
good fellowship among Weders and Danes.

    Unferth, the son of Ecglaf, spoke.
Sitting at the feet of the Scylding lord,   500
he sifted his words for the most contentious—
he found it an insult that Beowulf,
a foreign seafarer, should risk so much.
He could allow no man a notch of triumph
more on this earth than he himself: 505
"Are you that Beowulf who struggled with Breca,
risked the sea in a swimming match
where towering pride and reckless vaunt
placed you in harness to the waves themselves
and the fathomless water. No man,   510
neither friend nor foe, could curb the folly
of your setting forth alone, and on the sea.
There you two were on the ancient mother
thinking to measure her winding currents,
flyspecks on her expanse. The ocean boiled,   515
winter huge. Seven nights
you labored in her coils. He bested you at swimming,
had greater strength. Come morning the sea
bore him away to the Heathobards.
He turned homeward then to his own country,   520
his beloved people, the land of the Brondings,
the lovely stronghold where he had kinsmen,
domain and treasure. He made good
his boast on you, the son of Beanstan.
So I look for a worse outcome—   525
though granted you've held your own
in a few skirmishes—if you dare wait
the length of one night near Grendel."
    Beowulf spoke, the son of Ecgtheow:
"What a deal of nonsense, drunk with beer,   530
my good Unferth, you've said concerning
Breca's exploits. Let me set the record
straight: I had more strength on the sea,
and hardship too, than any other man.
We made a pact, as boys will sometimes—   535
we were both then scarcely bearded,
unseasoned youths—that we would hazard
our lives on the ocean, and so we did.
Hard in our hands, we held naked swords
as we stepped into the breakers. By them we hoped   540
to ward off the whale-fish. He could not swim

from me on the boiling waves, could not
outpace me at all, nor would I leave him.
We were together at sea the space
545 of five nights, until the flood drove us apart,
weltering waters, coldest weathers,
nights darkening and the wind howling
out of the north, the waves wolf-hearted.
Even the sea-fish were stirred up in spirit.
550 Against that peril, my life-sheathing garment
did its office—my war-shirt woven
and worked with gold lay on my breast,
each ring locked hard. A savage thing
dragged me to the sea-bottom, had me fast
555 in its grip. Yet it was granted
I should reach the evil being
with my sword-point: slaughter took
the huge sea-beast through my hand.

"So those vicious monsters tormented me
560 time and again. I served them in turn
with my good sword, as was fitting.
Those wicked sea-wolves had little joy
in the scrap they had from my hand
there on the sea-floor, their banquet board;
565 but in the morning they lay belly up
by the sea's other dead, their staring eyes
shut by a sword: no more would they hinder
the passage of sailors on the sea's
broad highways. Light came from the east,
570 God's bright beacon, the water grew wondrous calm
so that I saw windy sea-walls
and steep headlands. Wyrd often spares
the man unmarked by death if his courage holds.
Yet it so turned out I slew with my sword
575 nine sea-beasts. I've heard no other tale
of such night-combat under heaven's vault—
none so fierce, nor steeped so in hardship!
Somehow I survived those hostile talons,
though exhausted by the trial. The sea took me then,
580 the weltering surge carried me in its currents
to the land of the Finns. No such tale of similar
struggle, of sword terror, has reached my ears
concerning you. Breca never yet—

nor you for that matter—has come near
equaling my exploits at battle-play   585
with blood-adorned swords—nor is it a cause for boast,
though you murdered in cold blood your brothers,
your closest kinsmen. You'll pay for this,
suffering in hell, despite your ready tongue.
I'll tell you a hard truth, son of Ecglaf—   590
Grendel, evil demon though he is, could never
have devised such torments for your lord,
nor worked such humiliation in Heorot,
if you were half so brave as you make out.
Instead he has found little to fear   595
and nothing to dread in your prowess with swords—
the vaunted courage of the Victory-Scyldings!
He exacts his levy, sparing none
of the Danish folk, takes his pleasures where he pleases,
puts them to sleep, and then feasts on the Spear-Danes,   600
dreading no combat. Soon I'll grant him
a taste of Geatish manhood, offer him
this hand in battle. Let him who may
go blithe to drink when the morning light
of another day—the sun through radiant cloud—   605
shines from the south over the sons of men."
   At this, the generous and grey-haired
warrior was glad. The King of the Bright-Danes
counted on such help. Protector of his people,
he reckoned how steadfast was the man's resolve.   610
   Music resumed and the laughter of men,
brave words were spoken. Wealtheow went forth,
Hrothgar's queen, ever mindful of courtesy.
In gold raiment she greeted the men in the hall,
and that gracious woman first gave the cup   615
to the East-Danes' lord and protector;
she urged him, as he was dear to his people,
to enjoy the evening. He took the gold-heavy
hall-cup in his hands and drank deeply.
That woman of the Helmings, so handsome in her rings,   620
and gifted with virtue, went around the floor
to youth and veteran, each in his turn,
serving them from the chalice, until she stood
before Beowulf with her cup of mead.
She greeted all the Geats and thanked God   625
with prudent words that her will had come to pass,

and she had found a man to trust
as a comfort for their scourge. That slaugher-fierce man
received the cup from Wealtheow.
630 Her words had fired him with a zeal for war.
Beowulf spoke, son of Ecgtheow:
"I call to mind what I resolved at my journey's
outset, at sea with my band of men—
that I would fully execute
635 your people's will, or may death seize me
fast in the fiend's grip. I shall acquit
myself with courage, or here will I bide
my final moments in the mead-hall."
These words pleased the woman well,
640 this pledge and boast. The gracious queen
went in gold raiment to sit by her lord.
   Again there arose a joyous clamor,
again bright music and the brave talk
keen on victory, until, of a sudden,
645 Healfdene's son said he would quit the hall
for the evening. He knew what the demon
had in mind, the slaughter he compassed
for that splendid hall, since first light that day:
when night deepened over all,
650 shrouding darkness, the creature would come,
gliding unseen. The company arose.
Hrothgar took his leave of Beowulf, addressed
him hurriedly, wished him health,
the stewardship of the hall, and added these words:
655 "I've never granted to any man,
since I could lift either hand or shield
the keeping of this hall, except now to you.
Have and hold it now, this best of halls,
be mindful of fame, make known your courage,
660 watch for the demon. You will lack nothing
if your courage lasts, and your life with it!"

   Then Hrothgar, Protector of the Scyldings, with all
his men-at-arms, left the hall:
the chieftain sought Wealtheow's side,
665 his queen and bed companion. God in His glory
had decreed—so men had heard—
that one kept guard for Grendel, did strange
duty—giant-watch—for the Danish lord.

The man of the Geats devoutly trusted
in the strength of his great spirit, and the Lord's grace. 670
Then he removed his coat of mail,
and the helmet from his head, entrusted his sword,
that keenest of blades, to one who stood by,
and commanded him to guard the war-gear.
Before he lay down on the bed, Beowulf 675
spoke these boast-words—
"I reckon myself no less capable
in close combat than Grendel does himself.
And so I will not use my sword
to take his life, though I might do this. 680
He does not know that by such means
he could slay me, piercing my shield,
famed though he be for slaughter. We two
will forego the use of swords, weaponless
in combat, if he dare, and God in His wisdom 685
will afterward decide, as He thinks fitting,
into which hand he will award the spoils."
The brave veteran lay down, the pillow received
the valiant's countenance; around him
many stalwart sea-men took their rest. 690
Not one had hope of leaving there
to seek his home again, neither his kinfolk
nor the fair town where he spent his youth.
But they had heard how violent death
had swept away so many Danes 695
in that mead-hall. Yet the Lord gave
good fortune and war-luck—both comfort and succor—
to the Weders—thus were they able
to overcome the enemy through one man's strength
and splendid prowess. It is a truth well known 700
that mighty God held sway over men
then as now.
             By night, came gliding
that walker in darkness. The bowmen slept—
those set to guard the horn-gabled house— 705
all but one. It was known to men
that he lacked the power, when God put forth
His will, to drag them down to darkness—
for one kept watch in hatred for his foe,
rigid with anger, awaited what would come.
    He came from barren lands, under slopes breathing 710

mist—Grendel walking, despised by God.
The vicious killer planned to ensnare
a certain man in that high hall.
He crept under the heavens until the great building
715 glittered before him, the warrior's hall
hammered with gold. Nor was it
the first time he had visited Hrothgar's home:
but never had he found such a harsh reception—
fierce hall-guard, and the hardest of men.
720 That creature cut off from every joy
approached the hall. At once, at a single touch,
the fire-locked bands of the door gave way:
fiercely enraged, the evil thing swung wide
the hall's mouth. Quickly, he moved
725 inside, treading the beautiful mosaic
angrily underfoot. From his eyes gleamed forth
an unfair light, brilliant as fire.
Within the hall he saw many warriors
asleep together. He laughed to himself:
730 in his mind's eye, he saw the life of each man
husked from its body, and he, the vicious
banqueter, squatting at daybreak, his vast
appetite fully sated. It was not meant to be
that he would feast again on human flesh
735 after that night. Firm in his strength,
the kinsman of Higelac studied his every move,
guessing his reaction to a sudden attack.
Nor did the demon keep him in suspense;
740 without delay he seized the first
sleeping victim, slit the bones
from their coverings, guzzled the hot blood
straight from the veins, took huge bites,
gobbling down both hands and feet,
745 each morsel of the man. Then he stepped nearer
and seized with his claw the strong-hearted
man where he lay, the fiend would have him
pinned in his grip; instead his foe held him
with hostile intent, and pulled him down.
750 That keeper of sin soon found out
none had a stronger hand-grip than he,
no other man on Middle-Earth,
its furthest fields. He became afraid
for the first time: he could not move.

He had one thought: flee to his den 755
and his ally devils; this meeting was outside
his experience, unlike anything in his life before.
Then the great-hearted kinsman of Higelac
remembered his promise, rose to his full height,
gripping him tighter. Fingerbones broke: 760
the giant pulled away, the man came after.
The infamous thing intended, if he could,
to break free and then make off
to his lair in the marsh. He knew his fingers
gripped by his enemy: the vicious killer 765
counted it his hardest journey to Heorot.
The hall resounded; to each of the Danes,
and those outside the stronghold, even the most stern,
it seemed a harrowing banquet. Both hall-guards
were feverish with hatred. Their wrestling 770
shook the room. Men marvelled the wine-hall
could withstand such brutal use, that the fair house
did not fall to earth. But inside
and out, cunning smiths had braced it
with iron bands. There, where the hostile 775
combatants grappled, mead-benches with their gold
adornments were torn from the floor.
It had never occurred to the Scylding counselors
that a man could wreck that hall,
tear it asunder by any craft, that excellent 780
building adorned with bone, unless fire
should reach there and swallow it. The strange clamor
echoed repeatedly: to the North-Danes,
and those thronged about the walls,
and heard the weeping, it seemed a deep 785
horror. God's enemy, the bondsman of hell,
cried out from pain and loss. He sang
a terror song, held fast by one
unmatched in strength by any mortal
in the days of this life. 790

 The stern guardsman would not allow
the deadly guest to depart alive,
nor was his existence counted a blessing
by any man. Beowulf's warriors 795
time and again brandished their ancient swords,
they would stand between their leader and death,

protect their lord, if it lay in their power.
They did not know, those stern-minded swordsmen
who must endure the struggle, thrusting
800 from either side, thinking to reach
the creature's life: the evil thing
was invulnerable to any war-sword,
the finest steel could not scratch it;
he had cast a spell on hammered metals,
805 a trance lay on every blade. Little that availed
him as mortal creature, he must endure
the wretchedness of his going hence,
the solitude of his far journey
into the devil's power. He soon found out,
810 that one who fought with God, and was a canker
and vicious sore to the spirits of men,
that his body no longer served him—
the powerful kinsman of Higelac
gripped him by the hand. Each was to the other
815 death incarnate. The unappeasable demon
knew mortal pain: on his shoulder
a huge gash appeared, vein and sinew
were torn from the bone. To Beowulf was granted
glory in battle, and Grendel overcome.
820 Life-sick, he must flee to cloudy uplands,
seek his joyless home. He could be sure
he stood on his life's verge and precipice,
the last of his days. After the battle,
each Dane was satisfied. He who had come
825 so far, large in strength and wisdom,
had cleansed Hrothgar's hall, and cast
out the ruiner. He exulted in his nightwork,
the extent of his courage. He had carried out
all he had promised to the East-Danes,
830 and brought an end to their affliction,
cured the sickness they before had suffered
and must endure, constrained by sad necessity,
no minor woe. That was a token to behold—
after the brave one nailed up its hand,
835 arm and shoulder—there hung, entire,
Grendel's claw under the wide eaves of Heorot.

That morning, I have heard, many warriors
thronged about the gift-hall, chieftains

came from far and near, hazarding long journeys,
to look upon the wonder, and study the footprints 840
of their enemy. None considered it sad—
not one who gazed upon those tracks—
that he must die, the humbled thing,
crawling to the sea and its bestial shapes,
overcome by slaughter, bearing his blood-rimmed 845
footprints to the verge where all is forfeit.
There the sea welled with gore,
waves all stained with it, churning together,
surging with hot blood and battle oozings.
Bereft of all joy and doomed to die, 850
he hid himself in the depths of the marsh,
laid down his heathen soul: there hell received him.

    Old comrades in arms, and young men too,
went there afterwards, riding for pleasure
to the mere and back, mounted warriors 855
galloping on grey horses. All praised
Beowulf's achievement; said time and again
there was no better shieldbearer,
nor any more worthy of ruling a kingdom,
south or north under heaven's compass, 860
and along the endless strands of the sea.
Nor had they cause to reproach Hrothgar,
that radiant lord: he was a good king.
At times, they gave their horses free rein,
the warriors raced their glistening mounts 865
where they thought the country fair, on familiar
bridle-paths. At times, the king's thane,
a man laden with memory's riches
who could call to mind a great many
of the ancient stories, spun new garments 870
from the old cloth. Soon he began
to sing of Beowulf, skillfully recite
his recent exploits, weave his words
in an apt tale. Then he turned to the matter
of Sigemund, said all he had heard 875
concerning the courage of Wael's son,
of his far travels, and fierce encounters,
his feuds and crimes, which few men
had ever heard of, except Fitela
who had been at his side in many battles, 880
a trusted comrade and nephew to whom

he would speak of those close things.
A great many of the race of giants
had fallen under their swords. No little glory
885   was meted out to Sigemund after his death,
as a consequence of his killing the dragon,
hoarder of gold. He stepped under
the grey stone, the son of princes ventured
alone into its barrow, nor was Fitela with him.
890   Yet it so befell his sword pierced
the marvellous wyrm, that excellent iron
struck through it to the wall; the dragon succumbed.
The hero had acted with flawless courage,
so the ring-hoard was his to do with
895   as he desired; the son of Wael
loaded a sea-going boat, bore to its hold
the bright treasure; the dragon dissolved in flames.
    He was the most famous of exiles,
a protector of warriors, acknowledged among men
900   for his valorous deeds, his remarkable strength—
after Heremod's struggles came to an end,
he eclipsed that hero. This other had bitter luck—
betrayed among giants into the devil's power,
then quickly dispatched. He had been prey
905   to fits of choler too long, had become
a life-burden to noble and serf alike.
In earlier days, many counselors
had grieved the going forth of the resolute man.
They had counted on him for a cure of their woes,
910   that he should achieve a vigorous manhood,
a princely splendor, ruling his folk,
hoard and stronghold, a hero's realm,
the Scyldings' demesne. Such a man was Higelac's
kinsman, he had become a precious friend
915   to all mankind; this other sin possessed.
    Headlong over the cobbled streets,
they spurred their horses. The morning light
was hurrying as well. Many great-hearted men
had come to the fairest of halls
920   to see the cunning wonder. The king himself,
radiant keeper of the golden rings,
renowned in excellence, stepped in his glory
from the bridal chamber, walked to the mead-hall,
his queen at his side, and a throng of young girls.

    Hrothgar spoke at the hall's threshold,   925
after contemplating for a time the roof
of hammered gold and Grendel's claw:
"May the All-Wielder be thanked for this
fair sight. I have suffered unspeakable griefs
from Grendel. Yet God works wonder   930
after wonder always, Keeper of the world.
A short time ago, I was sure our sickness
would never end, no cleansing come
in all my days: when this best of halls
was running with blood, rank with battle-oozings—   935
a grief afflicting the springs of action
so none believed defense was possible
against those vicious devils and demons
besieging our stronghold. Through God's might,
a warrior has done what we could not,   940
for all our scheming, accomplish before.
Indeed the maiden who delivered that child
into the world can say, if yet
she lives, that God revealed
a singular grace at her child-birth.   945
Now Beowulf, best of men, I will hold
you in my heart as I would a son.
Conduct yourself with this new kinship
clearly in mind. Nor want for any
worldly good in my power to command.   950
Many a time have I rewarded lesser acts,
heaped honors on a humbler man
of more limited prowess. By your own hand
have you secured undying
glory. May the All-Wielder   955
grant you always such good as He did just now."
    Beowulf spoke, the son of Ecgtheow:
"Gladly we did that work of courage,
risked all in battle, assaying his
unknown strength. I would far rather   960
the creature itself was yours to see,
the demon in all its gear, strengthless from slaughter.
I planned to take him by surprise, bind him
with these two hands on the bed of death,
there watch his life ebb away,   965
and would have, but his body slipped free,
I couldn't keep him from going, cleave as closely

to my life-foe as I would; nor did God
allow it; the fiend's urge to be gone
970   was all too great. Yet he ransomed himself
with this hand, gave up both arm and shoulder
for the sake of his life. The luckless creature
could buy no remedy with that desperate act.
He will not live long oppressed by sin:
975   pain has narrowly compassed him,
necessity keeps him in stern bondage.
There that being in the rags of its mortal acts
must await the Last Judgment,
how bright God will deal with him."
980   Then the son of Ecglaf had little to say
about his prowess in battle
once he had gazed on that palpable evidence
of the man's strength—there, over the roof-beam
the demon's hand and fingers; from in front,
985   each nail and socket, the entire hand-spur
of the vicious demon, was just like steel—
a deadly spike. They all agreed
that not even the hardest of ancient swords
could leave a mark there, damage in the least
990   the monster's blood-mottled war-claw.
    Straightway, it was commanded that Heorot
be adorned within; both men and women
set to work making the wine-hall
fit for guests. Gold weavings
995   shimmered on the walls, men who studied them
saw wondrous figures gliding there.
That bright structure fastened with iron
bands was shattered within, its hinges cracked
and gaping; the roof alone unscathed
1000 after the demon reeking of evil
turned about in desperate flight,
despairing of survival. Nor is it easy—
do whatever he will—for a man to flee,
but as he possesses a soul and walks upon the earth,
1005 child of the clay he treads, necessity
compels him to search out the readied place
where, fast in its deathbed, his body
sleeps after the feast.
                    The moment arrived
when Healfdene's son entered the hall,

the king himself wished to share the feast. 1010
I have not heard of a greater band,
more courteous in bearing toward their lord.
Those famous men settled themselves along the bench
rejoicing in the banquet. The great-hearted kinsmen,
Hrothgar and Hrothulf, emptied their mead-cups 1015
with quiet ceremony in the high hall.
Heorot was thronged inside with friends.
The Scyldings were untouched at that time
by treacherous words. The son of Healfdene
then gave to Beowulf a battle-ensign— 1020
a golden standard—a helmet and a coat of mail,
in remembrance of his victory.
Many gazed on as the jewelled sword
was laid before him. Beowulf drank
from the hall-cup. He was not the least shamed 1025
before his men-at-arms by that granting of treasure.
I have never heard of any man
so gracious as he bequeathed at banquet
four such treasures worked with gold.
At the crest of the helmet, a metal ridge 1030
wound about with wires served as protection
to turn the edges of deadly swords
in the shower of battle, when, bearing his shield,
he must go forth against his enemy.
The protector of men ordered eight horses 1035
with gold-hammered cheek-guards be led
along the floor. Among them was one
with jewel-encrusted saddle, the king's
war-seat studded with precious stones
when the son of Healfdene would ride among 1040
the tossing sword-points—not once at the forefront,
in the midst of carnage, had the famous warrior yielded.
The protector of the Ingwines granted Beowulf
possession of both horse and weapon;
commanded him to use them well. 1045
That famous guardian of ancestral gold
repaid the combat with great munificence—
jewels and horses. None could censure him
who valued truth in the least.

Then the lord of men shared out treasures 1050
and ancient heirlooms to each of those

who accompanied Beowulf on the sea-voyage,
and ordered gold weighed out
as wergild for the warrior whom Grendel
1055 had savagely slain, as he would have others,
if God's wisdom and the workings of wyrd
had not stood in his way, and one man's will.
The Shaper ruled all men, then as now.
Therefore is understanding always best,
1060 and prudence of spirit. Those who abide in the world
any length of time these troubled days
must eat their portion of joy and pain.
    Again music and song were mingled together
in the presence of the Halfdanes' commander;
1065 the harp was struck again, and stories recalled
when it came time for Hrothgar's scop
to frame a fitting hall-entertainment—
he sang of the sudden attack when Finn's
retainers, and Hnaef of the Scyldings,
1070 all fell in Frisian slaughter.
    Hildeburh had little cause to praise the Jutes'
oath-keeping. Guiltless she suffered
the loss of dear ones—both brother and son—
when their shields met. Fated they fell,
1075 wounded by spears. That woman knew pain.
Those were not spendthrift tears
that Hoce's daughter shed, once morning came,
the radiance of dawn, and she could see
her murdered kinsmen, whom she had once held
1080 her portion of joy. War had taken
Finn's retainers, all but a few—
he hadn't the strength to press Hengest
any further on that battle-field,
those spared by the slaughter could not dislodge
1085 the prince's thane. So they tendered him
peace terms, promised him both hall and throne
which he could share and half control
with the band of Jutes,
and the son of Folcwalda would exalt the Danes
1090 time and again by his granting of treasure,
honor Hengest and his men with rings;
no less than his liege-men in the mead-hall,
they would receive precious encouragement,
bracelets and cups of hammered gold.

So on both sides pledges were sworn 1095
to keep peace. Famed for courage,
Finn concluded with an oath to Hengest
he would treat those spared by the slaughter
with all courtesy, as his counselors recommended—
providing no man violated the peace 1100
in word or deed, or falsely scheming,
ever complained, though they serve the slayer
of their ring-giver, as lordless they must.
Therefore, if any Frisian in rash quarrel
called to mind that murderous hatred 1105
the sword's edge must settle it.
A bonfire was built, and ancient gold
out of the hoard heaped there. The foremost warrior
of the Battle-Scyldings was laid in the flames.
Easy to see in that bonfire 1110
were blood-streaked coats of mail,
iron-hard swine-crests—gilt boar-images—
and the butchered men; no few had fallen!
Hildeburh commanded that her own son
be consigned to the flames of Hnaef's pyre, 1115
placed at his uncle's side, all his flesh
be consumed by fire. That woman wept,
keened in her grief. The warrior rose.
Coiled heavenwards that greatest of corpse-fires,
thundering by the mounds; skulls melted, 1120
wound-gates burst open, blood spurted
from severed veins. Fire, most greedy of spirits,
swallowed all whom war had taken
on either hand; their glory vanished on the wind.

    They hastened away, the warriors went home, 1125
bereft of friends, they dispersed into Frisia,
their halls and high demesne. Hengest yet
stayed with Finn that slaughter-stained
winter against his will; remembered his homeland
though he could not pilot his ring-prowed 1130
ship on the sea—it boiled with storms,
strove against wind; winter locked the shore-waves
in shackles of ice—until a new year
came again to that coast—as time out of mind
it always has, the luminous weather 1135
keeping the seasons. Winter was gone,

the home-fields fair. The exile hungered
to be gone from the hall. Yet his mind was set
on vengeance rather than sea-voyage—
1140 he intended to arrange a painful meeting
and remind the Jutes of the hardness of iron.
So he did not refuse the obligation
when Hunlaf's son laid in his lap
a glittering battle-sword, most excellent of blades.
1145 Its deadliness was well known among the Jutes.
By such means, bitter sword-death
was visited on Finn in his own hall—
once Guthlaf and Oslaf, after their sea-journey,
recalled the cruel slaughter, the grief that followed,
1150 and vented their pain. None could choke back
what must be spoken. Then the hall ran
with enemy blood, Finn was slain,
the king among his retinue, and the queen taken.
The victorious Scyldings carried to their ship
1155 all of the king's earthly possessions,
all they could find in Finn's home
of jewel-encrusted brooch. They carried that noble
wife as cargo, brought her home
to the Danish folk.   The tale was told,
1160 the singer's story at an end. Glad voices rang out once more,
the pleasant murmur of men at drink,
stewards poured wine from splendid cups.
Luminous in her gold, Wealtheow glided forth
to where nephew and uncle sat together; they were inseparable,
1165 each devoted to the other. And Unferth the orator
sat at the feet of the Scylding lord; they all trusted in his heart,
believed him possessed of great spirit, despite his ungentle usage
of close kinsmen in swordplay. Then the queen of the Scyldings
   said:
"Receive this cup, generous lord,
1170 distributor of jewels. Be in good spirits,
gold friend of warriors, and speak to our guests
with mild words, as a man ought.
Be gracious to the Geats, remember the wealth,
which, near and far, is yours to command.
1175 I was told you intend to adopt
this soldier as a son. Heorot is cleansed,
our bright gift-hall; be liberal with gold

so long as you can, and to your kinsmen leave
both kingdom and subjects, when you go forth
on your destined way. I know our gracious　　　　　　　　1180
Hrothulf well, trust he will show our sons
complete devotion, if you should leave
the world, friend of the Scyldings, before him.
I have no doubt he will requite our sons
with all kindness, if he calls to mind　　　　　　　　　　1185
the many favors we granted him, when still a boy,
to the increase of his honor and ambition."
She walked down the hall toward her sons,
Hrethric and Hrothmund, and the children of warriors,
all the youth together. There sat the good man,　　　　　1190
Beowulf of the Geats, beside the two brothers.

　　A cup was brought him, and their friendship
sealed with a drink, and braided gold
graciously presented—two bracelets,　　　　　　　　　　1195
chain mail and rings, and the fairest neck-collar
I have heard of on this earth—
no better remnant of warrior's hoard
under the radiant heavens, since Hama carried off
the Brosing necklace, and jewel and brooch　　　　　　　1200
to his own bright town. He fled Eormenric's
vicious deceit, chose eternal benefits.
Higelac of the Geats, the nephew of Swerting,
wore that neck-ring on his final adventure.
Under his battle-insignia he made his stand,
defended that heirloom, spoil of slaughter.　　　　　　　1205
His pride cost him his life, his fate
was to die in Frisia. That radiant lord
bore the collar of ancient stones
over the sea's chalice; then fell under his shield.
The king's body passed into Frankish hands　　　　　　　1210
and with it both necklace and coat of mail.
A lesser man stripped his corpse
after battle cut him down. The Geats were carrion
heaped on that field. The hall resounded.
Wealtheow spoke before the assembled men:　　　　　　　1215
"Enjoy this collar with all good fortune,
my dear young Beowulf, and this coat of mail,
ancient folk-treasure, is yours with my blessing,
make your strength known, and to these boys

1220 be kind in counsel. I will not forget these gifts.
You have brought it about that men will praise you
for a long time and far as the sea,
home of the winds, beats on headlands,
your name will be spoken. May you prosper
1225 so long as you live. I wish you increase
of earthly treasure. Treat my sons
as courtesy bids, and our remembered feasts!
Here each man is true to his fellow,
sweet in bearing, faithful to his lord,
1230 thanes share a single will, and their subjects obey them.
These feasting warriors do as I bid."
    She took her seat. Men drank their fill
at that best of feasts. They did not know
the hard fate shaped for them, as had befallen
1235 many before, when shadows lengthened,
and Hrothgar retired to his chamber,
the king to his rest. A great throng
guarded the hall, as often they did.
They cleared the benches and overspread them
1240 with pillows and bedding. A certain reveler
lay down to sleep whom death had marked.
They set their shields, their polished war-gear
over their heads. There on the bench
above the heroes firelight flickered
1245 on war-exalted helms, shirts of chain mail,
and thick spear-shafts. Such was their training
they were always ready to wage war,
whether at home or on campaign, as occasion
demanded and their lord had need.
1250 Those were experienced soldiers.

    Soon they fell asleep. One paid dearly
for his night's rest, as had often happened
when Grendel ruled the gold-hall
and worked evil, until death overcame him,
1255 a quelling of his sins. It soon was manifest
among men an avenger was yet at large,
and lived in torment for a time, nursing
her war-grief: Grendel's mother,
both woman and beast, gnawed her wound
1260 on the hell-cold sea bottom,
her fixed dwelling after Cain had slaughtered

his own brother, struck down
his closest kinsman. Cursed and branded
by murder, he fled all human fellowship,
haunted the wastelands. From him awoke   1265
the strain of demons of which Grendel was one—
wolf-hearted thing who found at Heorot
a man broad waking and ready for combat.
That demon locked him in a hard hand-grip;
yet he summoned every inch of his strength,   1270
the immense gift God had granted him,
and looked to the All-Wielder for assistance,
both comfort and courage. He overcame the creature,
vanquished the hell-spirit. Humbled, it fled;
cut off from every joy, the foe of mankind   1275
skulked off to die. And then his mother,
gluttonous and death-hungry, set out
on a painful journey to avenge her son.
   She came to Heorot where the Ring-Danes
were sleeping in their hall; as soon as Grendel's mother   1280
stepped over the threshold, a change in fortune
befell the men. The terror she invoked
was less than Grendel's by just so much
as a woman's strength is less than a warrior's
when the ancestral sword, beaten out by hammers,   1285
a blade steeped in blood and razor-keen
bites into the helmet's boar-image.
Many swords, unyielding of edge,
were drawn in that hall and broad shields
gripped firmly and lifted up. They didn't bother   1290
with helmet and mail when the terror seized them.
She had one thought: to escape quickly
and save her skin, when she found herself discovered.
Before any could act, she grabbed a warrior
fast in her claws as she fled to the marsh.   1295
He was Hrothgar's most valued retainer,
a man of proven courage, indispensable in war,
whose fame was destined to endure,
whom she plucked from sleep. Beowulf was absent,
the famous Geat had been assigned   1300
to a second chamber after the granting of treasure.
Screams rang through Heorot. She snatched the claw
covered in gore. Grief had struck again
those in the hall. Nor is it a good exchange

1305 when the blood of friends must be the coin
for settling accounts!
                    Sorrow overwhelmed
the wise king, the white-haired veteran,
when he learned his chief lieutenant lived no more,
his dearest friend was dead.
1310 Beowulf was summoned at once to the chamber.
Just at dawn the victorious man
came as bidden, the high-born champion
with his men-at-arms approached the king
whose mind was bent on a single question,
1315 would God ever grant an end to their woe?
Proud in his war-fame, he crossed the floor
with his men-at-arms—the hall resounded—
to stand before the lord of the Ingwins,
and address him, inquire if he had spent
1320 a pleasant night after their revels.

    Hrothgar spoke, the protector of the Scyldings:
"Do not speak of pleasure! Pain is come again
to the Danish folk. Aeschere is dead,
Yrmenlaf's elder brother,
1325 trusted counselor to whom my heart
was ever open, my comrade in war
when we shielded each other, as sword bit
into boar-crested helm. As a man ought to be
preeminent in courage so was Aeschere.
1330 It was his fate the ungovernable spirit
hovering in slaughter struck him down in Heorot.
I cannot say what path the demon—
pleased by her meal and gloating—has taken home.
Enough to say, she avenged your killing of Grendel
1335 night before last, when you tore him
with your bare hands, because he had preyed
on my people too long. He fell in battle,
his life forfeit; and now another mighty
man-killer has come to avenge her blood relative
1340 and has so repaid your fierce deed
that it is to many of my thanes—
those grieving apart after the gold-bestowal—
a heart-wrenching wound; now the hand is still
which might have granted your every wish.
1345   "Landholders among my people,

hall counselors, have informed me
they have seen two such huge
wanderers in the wastes, alien spirits
who rule the moors. So far as any man
can know such things, one of them 1350
appeared to be female. The other wretched creature
who walked in exile was manlike in shape—
except he was bigger than any living man.
Earth-dwellers in the earlier days
called him Grendel. They knew not 1355
who sired them, and whether they were the issue
of a whole race of such demons. They rule a secret realm—
wolf-trodden slopes, wind-swept headlands,
waste places where the waterfall
plunges downward in the ridge-shadow, 1360
a precipitous torrent. It is not far,
reckoned by miles, that dark water.
Over it hang trunks glazed in ice,
huge-rooted trees lean over the mere.
Men fear and marvel to see by night 1365
fire on that flood. Even the most far-seeing
of humankind cannot fathom that abyss.
Though the deer on the heath worried by hounds,
the strong-horned stag, will take to the holt,
pursued from afar, he will sooner forfeit, 1370
give up his life, than plunge from the bank
to save himself. That is no pleasant spot!
Billowing wavesmoke rises up
dark to the skies, and the wind begets
harsh weather, until clouds blacken, 1375
the heavens weep. The remedy once more
depends on you alone. You haven't yet seen
the hazardous ground where the sinful creature
has its dwelling; seek it, if you dare!
I'll reimburse you for your pains 1380
with ancient treasure—torques of gold—
as I did before, if you return alive."

   Beowulf spoke, the son of Ecgtheow:
"Do not mourn, prudent man! It is better always
to avenge a loss than brood overlong. 1385
For each of us an end must come
to our mortal life; we must labor for fame

A Translation of *Beowulf*

    'ore death takes us; that is afterwards best
    for the man-at-arms, his life spent.
1390 Rise up, protector of a kingdom, let us go forth
    and find these tracks of Grendel's kinswoman.
    I swear you this: she will find no haven,
    not in the bowels of the earth, nor mile-high forests,
    nor ocean's abyss—go where she will.
1395 Be at peace. Have patience this day
    for each of your woes, as I expect you will."
    The aged man sprang to his feet,
    thanked Almighty God for the man's resolve.
     A horse was bridled for Hrothgar,
1400 a mount with braided mane. The prudent king
    rode out in splendor; foot soldiers followed
    with heavy shields. Her tracks were seen
    all too easily along the woodland paths,
    her earth-cleaving tread, as she travelled straight
1405 over the dark moor, carrying the best
    of the young retainers—his lifeless body—
    that with Hrothgar had defended the homeland.
    The band of aethelings crossed on horseback
    steep talus slopes, narrow defiles
1410 where men go one by one, if at all,
    seaward-plunging headlands, and the haunts of sea-beasts.
    One of a handful, he went before them
    to scout the way into that country—
    wheeling in surprise, he saw grey stone
1415 grizzled with fir-trees, a joyless wood
    from cliff to shore; the water below
    blood-dark and turbulent. To each Dane there,
    every loyal friend of the Scyldings, each
    warrior, it was a wrenching of the spirit,
1420 a grief hard to bear, once they had seen
    the cliff where hung Aeschere's head.
    They saw waves veined with blood,
    warm upwellings of gore. A horn sang out
    with war-eager note. The foot-troop sat down.
1425 In the water they saw many kinds of serpents,
    marvellous snakes coiling as they swam,
    and beasts hauled out on the seaward ledges—
    such serpents and creatures which prey on ships
    sailing at dawn on the sea-routes.
1430 They plunged into the surf, enraged and bellowing—

they had heard the brazen clamor
of the war-horn. One of the Weders
loosed an arrow from his bow—that shaft
struck in the vitals, sheared a creature
of its wave-plundering life; it was more sluggish 1435
in its sea-swimming, whom death had overtaken.
With their war-hooked boar-spears
they grappled with it on the waves, dragged
it roughly on to the beach,
the wave-goer bristling with wonders. Men stared 1440
at the grisly thing.
     Beowulf put on
a hero's armor, gave no thought for his life;
that handwoven chain mail, clasped
and adorned with cunning, must hazard the sea—
it knew how to enfold his body 1445
so that searching talon and treacherous hand
could never scar his living breast;
protecting his head, the helmet of white silver
must disturb the ocean's muddy floor
and probe the sea-currents; it was studded with jewels, 1450
and lavished with metal bands, as long ago
the smith fashioned it, a thing to marvel at,
crested with boar images, so afterwards
no flashing blade or battle-sword could leave a mark there.
That was not the least of potent allies 1455
Hrothgar's advisor lent him in his need;
that hilted sword was named Hrunting,
it was the remnant of an ancient treasure;
its iron blade, hardened by slaughter-blood,
twisting with serpent-marks, was venomous as nightshade. 1460
It had failed none who had gripped it in battle,
wagered his life on dangerous campaigns,
on hostile fields; that was not the first time
it must prove its virtue in works of courage.
Indeed, the son of Ecglaf, immense in strength, 1465
did not remember what he had said before,
flushed with wine, when he loaned the weapon
to the superior swordsman; he did not dare
risk his life under the violent surf,
or test his metal; there he lost face, 1470
and a hero's fame. Such could not be said
of the other when he armed for combat.

       Beowulf spoke, the son of Ecgtheow:
       "Always remember, renowned son of Healfdene,
1475   farseeing prince, gold-friend of warriors,
       what we agreed upon, now that I am come
       to the verge of departure: if serving your need,
       I should forfeit my life, be always to me,
       absent on my way, as a father.
1480   Guard and cherish these young thanes,
       my heart's comrades, if battle takes me;
       and send to Higelac all the treasures
       that you gave me, beloved Hrothgar.
       The Lord of the Geats will know the moment
1485   he gazes on that gold, and contemplates that equipage,
       that I found a ring-giver preeminent
       in princely virtues, and enjoyed him while I might.
       To Unferth I would ask that you leave this heirloom,
       this stern blade patterned like the sea
1490   with spiralling waves. With Hrunting I will work
       enduring fame, or death will take me!"
          After those words, the man of the Weders
       hastened to be gone; he would not wait
       for any reply; the surges of the sea
1495   received the warrior. Part of a day passed
       before he could see the bottom of the abyss.
       Soon she discovered—that unappeasable demon
       who had ruled the reaches of the flood
       for half a century—that a certain man
1500   pierced her sanctum from above.
       She reached toward him, gripping the warrior
       in evil talons; yet they did not touch
       his living body; chain mail ensheathed it—
       she could not claw through that war-cloak,
1505   the locked meshes of the armor, with her hostile fingers.
       When she came to the bottom, the sea-wolf bore
       that prince in his armor to her own dwelling—
       despite his tremendous courage, he could not
       draw his weapon; instead he was hedged about
1510   by strange tormentors, sea-beasts
       tore at his mail with hostile tusks,
       demons plucked at him. Then the warrior perceived
       he was within a certain violent place
       where, nonetheless, water could not reach him,
1515   nor the flood's onslaught harm him in the least

because of that roofed hall. He saw firelight,
a brilliant flame burning there.
   Then the hero saw that cursed she of the abyss,
the sea-wife in her strength; he struck her a great blow
with his war-sword, spared her none of its edge   1520
so the ring-marked steel sang out against her skull
a brazen war-song. Her guest discovered
his flame-bright sword couldn't so much
as scratch her skin: the blade failed
the prince in his need; it had endured   1525
hand-to-hand combat, sheared helmet
and armor of the fated-to-die: this was the first time
that treasure's virtue had proved insufficient.
   The kinsman of Higelac again steeled himself—
unswerving in courage, mindful of glory;   1530
angrily he hurled the wave-shimmering sword
studded with gem-stones, so it stuck in the ooze,
firm and steel-edged. He trusted in his strength,
his powerful hand-grip. So must a man act
if he intends to gain immortal glory   1535
in the press of battle; he scorns his very life.
The man of the Geats seized Grendel's mother
by the shoulder—he didn't regret the struggle—;
swollen with rage, the war-hardened one
threw his life-foe so she fell to the floor.   1540
She wasted no time in repaying the favor
with hard hand-locks, clutching him to her.
Overcome by weariness, the strongest of warriors
stumbled on his feet and fell.
She straddled the hall-guest, and unsheathed her thick   1545
and shimmering dagger; she would avenge her son,
her only offspring. On his breast lay
the braided mail; it guarded his life,
prevented the entry of edge or point.
The son of Ecgtheow, champion of the Geats,   1550
would have journeyed to his doom under the wide earth
had not his battle armor protected him,
his hard war-mesh—and holy God
saw to his victory; all-knowing Lord,
Heaven's Monarch, easily brought about   1555
the just outcomĕ, so he again stood.
   He saw among the equipage, the victory-annointed blade,
the heirloom of giants unyielding of edge,

the wage of heroes; that was the best of weapons
1560 though so huge and heavy no other man
could wield it in the thick of battle,
that jewelled and luminous work of giants.
The madness of battle on him, the Scylding
man grabbed the hilt-chain, drew forth
1565 that ring-marked blade and angrily struck
so that her neck shivered from the blow,
her vertebrae snapped. The edge sliced
her death-bitten flesh; she slumped to the floor;
the sword was blood-soaked, the man exultant.
1570   Light kindled there, a radiance blazed forth
just as heaven's candle beacons clearly
from the firmament. He scanned the hall;
angry and resolute, Higelac's thane
stalked along the floor, the lifted sword
1575 clenched in his hand—that blade was not
a burden to him—now, without delay,
he would avenge Grendel's butchery,
the slaughter accomplished against the West-Danes
far more often than a single time
1580 when he wrenched from sleep Hrothgar's friends
and kinsmen, wakened only to die
fifteen men of the Danish folk,
and made off with many others,
an unspeakable sacrifice! He paid him back in kind,
1585 the merciless champion, when he saw Grendel
himself asleep, exhausted by slaughter,
lifeless from the wounds dealt him before
in combat at Heorot. The body jerked
under the sharp blow, the brutal war-stroke
1590 it suffered after death, then he severed its head.
   Soon the wise counselors, who with Hrothgar
kept watch on the water, saw the violent surf
lashing more wildly, the salt sea
boiling with blood. The ancient grey-haired
1595 advisors about Hrothgar spoke with one voice—
they did not reckon the aetheling would return,
exultant with victory carrying trophies
to his great lord; many judged
the sea-hag had broken him.
1600 The day wore on. The valiant Scyldings
withdrew from the headland; the gold-friend of warriors

turned homeward then. Their guests remained,
sick at heart, and stared on the water;
they hoped without hope their beloved lord
would appear from the depths. Then the sword drenched 1605
in war-blood began to dwindle
into long strips like icicles—it was a great marvel
that it would melt in the manner of ice
as when the Father loosens the bonds of frost,
unfastens the shackles that bind the deep— 1610
He who has dominion over the days and years,
the true Ordainer. The man of the Geats
took no more of those treasures—though he saw many there—
than the severed head along with the hilt
studded with gem-stones; the wave-marked blade 1615
had been consumed by fire, so hot was that blood,
so venomous the interloper who had died there.
He who had seen the hostile creatures
vanquished in battle dove up through the water.
The turbulent waves were all cleansed, 1620
the wide gulfs, when the interloper
relinquished her life and this loaned earth.
    The master of the sea-men, dauntless spirit,
swam to land. He joyed in the sea-plunder,
the enormous burden he bore in his arms. 1625
Exultant, the brave handful of thanes
clustered about him, thanked God
he stood before them alive and well.
Quickly, they relieved the capable man
of helmet and mail. The waves grew still, 1630
that water under the heavens running with blood.
They set forth along the footpaths,
blithe in spirit, made their way
to familiar roads. Royal in courage,
they carried the head from seaward cliffs, 1635
a hard task for each of them,
despite their willing spirits; four must shoulder
the heavy war-shaft, bear the burden
of Grendel's head to the gold-hall,
until, of a sudden, they arrived at Heorot, 1640
their valor proven by war, fourteen of the Weders
going on foot, their lord among them,
treading the meadows beside the mead-hall.
The thanes' commander stepped inside,

1645 the valiant man covered in glory,
fearless in battle, greeted Hrothgar.
Grendel's head was dragged by its hair
into the hall where men were drinking—
a ghastly spectacle quailing the heart
1650 before the men and their queen; struck dumb, they stared.

Beowulf spoke, the son of Ecgtheow:
"Behold this sea-gift, son of Healfdene,
leader of the Scyldings, we have willingly brought you,
this token of triumph you gaze upon.
1655 Not with ease, I emerged alive
from my struggle beneath the verge—I gained my victory
at some expense; the combat would have come
to a quick ending had God not shielded me.
Wielding Hrunting at war, I still
1660 could accomplish nothing, despite the weapon's excellence.
Yet the Ruler of men directed my gaze
to the wall where hung a beautiful
ancient broadsword—He often favors
the solitary man—so I unsheathed the weapon.
1665 When the occasion allowed, I struck her down in battle,
the keeper of that house. Then the wave-marked war-sword
burned to a cinder when blood fell upon it,
scorching battle-sweat. I carried the hilt
away from the demons; avenged their evil deeds,
1670 the slaughter of Danes, as was fitting.
I swear you may sleep in Heorot
ungrieving this night with your company of men,
with each of your subjects, your men-at-arms,
veterans and youths. You need harbor no fear,
1675 lord of the Scyldings, for your part,
that any harm will touch them, as you did before."
    Then the golden hilt, forged by giants long ago,
was laid in the hand of the ancient one,
the grey-haired king; after the devils' fall,
1680 it came into the possession of the Danish lord,
this work of cunning smiths; the cruel-hearted creature
God's foe, relinquished the world,
guilty of murder, and his mother as well;
it came into the power of the most excellent prince,
1685 the best of those between two oceans
who dealt out rings in Denmark.

    Hrothgar spoke—he studied the hilt,
the old heirloom, inscribed with the beginning
of the ancient feud, when the flood, the streaming
ocean, annihilated the giants' brood,   1690
visited them with terror. That tribe was estranged
from the Eternal Lord. He gave them
their final payment in the engulfing water.
The hilt-guard was clearly lettered
with runes etched in radiant gold,   1695
saying for whom the sword was first forged,
that keenest of blades, and the lacework of its hilt
coiled with serpents. Then the wise one spoke,
the son of Healfdene—the hall fell silent:
"He who frames his words with a care for truth   1700
and, steward of the past, summons to mind
ancient standards, can say this man
was nobly born. Your name is exalted
to the ends of the earth, made luminous in every land,
my dear Beowulf. You cleaved to your purpose,   1705
relied on prudence no less than strength.
To you I shall extend the full measure of friendship,
and you shall be a prop and a stay
against your people's confusion.
                              Heremod was no such blessing   1710
to the descendants of Ecgwela, the Glory-Scyldings.
As he grew to manhood, he brought the Danes
no joy but death, and fields of carnage;
in his fits of choler, he cut down his hearth-companions,
his comrades in battle, and the great lord
passed alone from human fellowship   1715
though the Almighty Lord had raised him up in strength,
exalted him above all other men
with a more than human might. Yet his heart grew
vicious and hard; he withheld the rings
that reward triumph. Joyless, he lived   1720
and suffered for the feuds he had fathered,
a lifelong torment. Learn from this
how a prince should live. Wise in winters,
I say this for your sake.
                                      It is awesome to contemplate
how the Lord God through his vast conception   1725
grants wisdom to some, and to others
titles and lands; He oversees all things.

At times He allows that a man be absorbed
by pleasure alone; grants him his heart's desire
1730 of earthly treasure, the rule of populous
harbors and towns; places in his hands
control of commonwealths and vast kingdoms—
the world possesses him, in his folly
he can't conceive he will ever die.
1735 His life is one long feast, neither sickness
nor age disturbs him nor bitter care
darkens his heart, nor does contention demand
a settlement by sword—for him the world
is a spinning toy; he can imagine nothing else—
1740 until vaunting pride mounts up within him,
takes root in his heart; then the guard slumbers,
the soul's keeper; that sleep is too sound,
obsessed with trifles, the slayer lurks near
who shoots from his bow all wickedness.
1745 Then he is struck beneath his helmet, there in his breast
by this bitter shaft—he can summon no protection
from the twisted biddings of the accursed spirit;
he deems the years he ruled too fleeting,
his bloated heart yearns for more, he gives
1750 no hammered gold, and forgets entirely
the future estate ordained by God,
the Lord of creation, his glory in heaven.
Afterwards, it inevitably happens
that the body, loaned as it is, must wither
1755 and foredoomed, die; another succeeds him,
a spendthrift who gives away treasure,
ancestral heirlooms, heedless of evil.
Gird yourself against wickedness, dear Beowulf,
best of men, and choose what is true,
1760 the eternal gifts; forego pride,
famous champion. The fulness of your strength
lasts but a while; it soon will happen
that sickness or the sword's edge will part you from life,
fire will reach for you or the engulfing flood,
1765 or the grip of iron, or the spear's flight,
or festering age; or the brightness of your eyes
be quenched in night; it will come, and quickly,
warrior, death will cut you down.
  "So I ruled the Ring-Danes for fifty winters
1770 beneath the heavens, with spear and sword

staved off war from many tribes
throughout Middle-Earth so that no one
under the arching sky dare count me a foe.
Yet here in my own realm, a reversal came,
grief after gladness, once Grendel, that ancient 1775
adversary stepped across my threshold;
I carried that persecution, a torment in my heart,
for a long time. May the Ordainer be thanked,
the eternal Lord, that I have lived to see
with my own eyes this head dripping with blood 1780
after our long struggle. Go now to your seat,
enjoy to the full this pleasant feast,
war-famed champion; when morning comes
we will share a great many gifts."
  The Geat was gladdened, went straightway 1785
to take his seat, as the wise one had asked.
As fairly as before, a feast was prepared,
a new entertainment for the seated men,
the famed-for-courage. Night's shroud
darkened about them. The veterans arose; 1790
the grey-haired king, ancient Scylding,
sought his bed. The Geat, the brave
shieldbearer, had measureless longing for sleep—
that voyager from afar, wearied by combat,
was shown his quarters by an attendant thane 1795
who out of courtesy provided for all
the thanes' comforts, as in those days
men on campaign were accustomed to.
  The great-hearted man rested; the hall rose up
steep and gold-adorned; the guest slept within 1800
until the black raven greeted sunrise
with a blithe heart. Light quickly banished
the last of the shadows. The warriors hastened,
the aethelings were eager to fare forth
to their own people; the proud visitor 1805
set his heart on taking ship.
  The bold one commanded that Hrunting,
that precious blade, be borne to Ecglaf's son.
He thanked him for the use of the sword,
said he reckoned it a good ally, 1810
effective in war, and did not fault
the weapon's edge; he was an excellent man.
And then the men-at-arms, equipped with war-gear,

were eager to be gone; honored among the Danes,
1815 a veteran tried in battle, the aetheling
approached the high seat, addressed Hrothgar:

    Beowulf spoke, the son of Ecgtheow:
"We seafarers come from afar
must now make known our resolve
1820 to return to Higelac. Here were we entertained
with royal courtesy: you were an excellent host.
If I can somehow gain even more
of your affection than I yet have,
lord of warriors, through my prowess at battle,
1825 I stand ready to be of service.
If word comes over the sea's expanse
that your neighbors threaten you with war,
as your enemies often have in times past,
I will bring you a thousand thanes
1830 as allies in your need. I am certain that Higelac,
the lord of the Geats, though still inexperienced
as leader of his people, would stand behind me
in word and deed, so my support would be most
tangible, and you should see lofty spears
1835 as proof of it, all that our strength can provide
for your want of men. If Hrethric, the king's son,
determines to visit the court of the Geats,
he will find friends there; travel to far countries
always profits the capable man."
1840   Hrothgar spoke to him in reply:
"The Lord in his wisdom has sent these words
into your mind; I have never heard
so young a man speak more wisely.
You are great in strength, prudent in spirit,
1845 and wise in discourse. It is my belief
that should it happen a spear strikes down
Hrethel's son in violent battle,
that sickness or sword takes your prince,
your people's leader, and you yet live,
1850 that the Sea-Geats could never choose
a more excellent king—hoard-guardian of men—
than you, if your desire be to rule
your kinsman's kingdom. Your character pleases me more
the longer I know it, beloved Beowulf.
1855 You have brought about among our kindred,

the Geatish people and the Spear-Danes,
a mutual alliance, and an end to bloodshed,
the treacherous enmities that plagued them before;
so long as I rule this wide kingdom
there shall be a sharing of treasure, men will greet   1860
one another with gifts across the gannet's bath,
ring-necked ships ride over the sea
with tokens of our love. I trust our peoples
will be of one mind toward friend and foe alike,
blameless in all respects, according to the old ways."   1865
   So the protector of men, son of Healfdene,
granted him twelve treasures;
he bade him go forth with those gifts
in safety to his own folk, and soon return.
Then the king kissed the good aetheling,   1870
the lord of the Scyldings held in his arms
the best thane; tears fell
from the grey-haired man. The ancient one
in his wisdom foresaw two outcomes
with one more likely: never again   1875
would they see one another, or confer in council.
He loved the man too well, and so he wept.
Chained fast in his breast by memory,
a deep longing for the dear man
burned in his blood. Beowulf went from him,   1880
the gold-radiant warrior trod the greensward,
exulting in treasure; the sea-traveller
rode at anchor, awaiting its captain.
They frequently praised Hrothgar's gifts
as they marched together; he was a king   1885
none could gainsay until age
stripped him of his strength, as it has so many.

   The band of young and valiant men-at-arms
reached the sea; they wore chain mail,   1890
shirts of woven steel. The shore-guard
scanned the returning soldiers, as before.
He did not hurl insults from the cliff-edge
at the visitors below, instead he galloped toward them,
said the warriors in bright armor approaching the ship
would be welcome to the Weder people.   1895
War-gear was stowed in the spacious hold,
jewels and horses brought aboard the ship

with its coiled prow; the mast towered
over Hrothgar's hoard-treasures.
1900 He gave the boat-guard a golden-hilted
sword, so afterwards he was reckoned
more richly dowered with ancient treasure
when he feasted with men. The hero departed,
his ship cut across deep channels, leaving behind
1905 the Danes' land. Sea-cloth was secured,
the mast rigged with sail; the kelson groaned;
wind over waves didn't hinder
the trim ship; with foam at its throat,
the voyager sped homeward over the waves,
1910 the coiled prow over the brimming sea,
until cliffs of the Weders, familiar headlands
cut the horizon; pitched forward by wind,
the keel scraped gravel, made landfall.
In a moment he was there, the harbor-guard
1915 who had kept the long vigil, constantly scanning
far out to sea for the beloved men.
The big-holded ship was moored to the beach
with stout anchor-ropes, so the wild surf
could not break asunder the lovely bark.
1920 He commanded the aetheling's treasure be carried
up from the ship—gold-encrusted swords and cups.
The ring-giver, Higelac Hrethel's son,
was not far to seek, the King residing
near the sea-cliffs, at court with his thanes.
1925   The stronghold was stately, and the valiant king
exalted on the throne beside his young queen.
Hygd, Haereth's daughter, was the model
of prudence, though yet inexperienced
in the ways of the world; even so, she was not close-fisted
1930 nor sparing of gifts—of magnificent treasures—
to her loyal subjects. Unlike Modthrytho:
famous queen who cowed her people
with her wickedness—none of her thanes
dare approach the woman, except her husband,
1935 to gaze upon her perilous beauty;
or he was destined for a tightly knit
death-collar, and immediately after
the dread hand on his shoulder, the sword was drawn,
the blade worked like beautiful cloth
1940 signalled his certain death. It is not queenly

for a woman to act so—however handsome she may be—
for a peace-weaver to pretend an insult
and so have put to death some dear man.
Hemming's kinsman brought an end to that—
a man said to his companion at drink 1945
she would be less of a grief to her people,
and a source of woe, once she was given
in gold raiment to the young champion,
the brave aetheling. Afterwards, as her father
had commanded, she sought Offa's hall 1950
over the fallow waves. Once there, she became
famous for her virtue on the folk-throne,
enjoyed, while she lived, what fate granted her,
drank the full measure of love with that prince—
the best, I have heard, of all mankind, 1955
of the myriad peoples beside the two seas.
Afterwards, Offa was known far and wide
through his gifts and victories, his good supply
of brave spear-men; he ruled his kingdom
wisely—from him descended Eomer, 1960
a friend of his people, Hemming's blood-kin,
grandson of Garmund, skilled in battle.

   The bold one set forth with his loyal band,
walked the sandy margin of the sea,
the windy beaches. World's candle shone, 1965
the sun high in the south; they had survived the journey,
and went in courage to that shield of men,
Ongentheow's killer, the young war-king
residing in his stronghold, as they had heard,
a generous ring-giver. Quickly Higelac 1970
was apprised of Beowulf's arrival,
that the protector of warriors—of shieldbearers—
had returned alive, unscathed from the combat,
and even that moment was approaching the hall.
Immediately, the floor within was cleared, 1975
as the king commanded, for the coming guests.
   He sat down beside him—he who had survived the struggles—
kinsman with kinsman, after he addressed
his sworn prince with great ceremony
and high speech. Haereth's daughter 1980
glided about the hall, carefully attending
the mens' comfort, handing the ale-cup

to each of the soldiers. Overcome by curiosity,
Higelac turned to his kinsman in the royal
1985 hall, inquired most courteously
of the adventures the Sea-Geats had had:
"What befell you on your journey, my dear Beowulf,
when, without warning, you made up your mind
to seek out a quarrel over the salt sea,
1990 this combat at Heorot? Did you find any cure
for Hrothgar's, that great lord's,
famous grief? Pain and foreboding
troubled my heart—I had no faith,
precious man, in your undertaking; I gave commands
1995 that you keep your distance from the slaughtering demon,
let the South-Danes themselves settle
this feud with Grendel. I thank God
you've made it back sound and whole."
   Beowulf spoke, the son of Ecgtheow:
2000 "Our great meeting, lord Higelac,
is scarcely a secret to many peoples—
such was the combat between Grendel and me
in that same place where unnumbered torments—
lifelong pain—had been his legacy
2005 to the Victory-Scyldings. I avenged that—
so none of Grendel's kinsmen who remain
alive on the earth, not one of that species
steeped in malice, has reason to boast
of our dawn-clamor. First I arrived
2010 at the ring-hall and greeted Hrothgar;
as soon as the great son of Healfdene
grasped my heart's resolve—my mind's thought—
he appointed me a seat by his sons.
His folk were feasting; never have I seen
2015 under heaven's vault more joyous fellowship
of men at drink. Now and again the famous queen,
covenant of peace, passed through the hall
encouraging her sons; several times she made gifts
of twisted rings before resuming her seat.
2020 Now and again, Hrothgar's daughter
served each man from a ceremonial cup.
I heard the men sitting in the hall
call her who carried the studded vessel
Freawaru—that gold-adorned girl

is promised to Froda's radiant son. 2025
The Scyldings' friend, protector of a kingdom,
has taken counsel and has been persuaded
the marriage will forestall a deadly feud,
ending slaughter. Seldom, however,
is the death-spear idle even a little while 2030
after a prince's fall, though the bride be fair.
  "The King of the Heathobards might well be angered,
and each of his attendant lords,
when the son of their enemy, his lady at his side,
crosses the floor to enjoy the feast. 2035
Glittering at his belt the heirloom hangs,
perilous blade of plaited iron,
treasure of the Heathobards for as long as they could
wield it—until they were lost at shield-play,
both sword and he who carried it. 2040
Then an old warrior bitten by memory
of one who had borne that lovely blade
and his slaughter by spear, his grieving mind
set on a grim path, begins to probe
his young lord's mind, incite 2045
him to revenge with these words:
'Are you blind, my friend, or do you not see
the sword your father bore into battle,
the precious blade, when last he went forth
in war-helmet, where the Danes slew him 2050
carrying the day on the corpse-field,
after Withergeld fell before the proud Scyldings?
Now one of those same killers' sons
flaunts those spoils and goes scot-free,
boasts of murder, and bears the prize 2055
which by rights should be yours to do your bidding.'
In such wise he calls to mind old wrongs
and with bitter words brings on the hour
when the woman's retainer lies laced in blood,
put to sleep by a sword, paying with his life 2060
for his father's deeds. His killer meanwhile
escapes alive, knowing the country.
Soon warriors' oaths are broken
by both tribes. Violent hatred
galls Ingeld; grief-racked, 2065
his love for his wife grows colder.

Therefore, I place no trust in any peace,
or proffer of friendship, however sincere,
from the Heathobards.
                    "Now shall I speak
2070 of Grendel that you may know,
my ring-giver, the outcome of heroes'
hand-grappling. After heaven's gem
glided to rest, a demon sought us,
a giant night-guest full of ire
2075 came to where we lay, guarding the hall.
There battle felled Hondscio,
claimed the fated man; he died first,
the soldier in his gear; Grendel became
the magnificent thane's mouth-slayer,
2080 every scrap of the man's body he swallowed.
Nor would the bloody-tusked butcher,
death-obsessed, go yet
empty-handed from the gold-hall.
The mighty one assayed my strength,
2085 his eager hand held me. A spacious pouch,
cunningly clasped, hung at his side;
ancient malice fashioned it,
the cunning of devils from dragon skins.
Inside that, the merciless killer
2090 wished to thrust me, unsinning,
as he had so many. He could not,
once I stood up, hot with anger.
It is a long story to say how I repaid
that predator on men for his every evil;
2095 these deeds, my lord, brought increase
of honor to your folk. He fled away,
to enjoy his life but a little while;
yet he left behind a reminder of his visit,
his right hand in Heorot, and abject then,
2100 grieving in spirit, sank to the sea bottom.
The lord of the Scyldings repaid my pains
with an abundance of gold cups,
many treasures, once morning came
and we sat down to banquet again.
2105 Voices rose in song, an ancient Scylding
of keen memory told of long ago.
At times the brave veteran stroked the harp,
released joy from the light wood,

at times he recited a sad tale,
at times the great-hearted king recalled 2110
marvellous adventures; then, bent with age,
he mourned his youth, his vanished war-strength.
Grief unmanned him, wise though he was,
when he remembered how it once had been.
We took our pleasures the livelong day 2115
inside the hall, until night returned
once more to men. Grendel's mother
hungered for revenge, set out quickly
on her sad journey. Death—a Weder's
anger—had swept her son away. 2120
The monstrous woman avenged her son,
slain by valor. Aeschere followed,
prized counselor, his life snuffed out.
After morning came, the death-wearied
Danish people could do nothing 2125
for the dear man—neither cremate him,
nor place him on a pyre; she carried his corpse
in her cruel talons under a mountain torrent.
That was the bitterest loss Hrothgar had suffered
for a long while. By your life, lord, 2130
the grief-stricken king implored me
to risk my life, test my courage
in the violent surf, gaining thereby
lasting glory. He promised me gifts.
It is widely known I found her beneath the flood, 2135
the grim keeper of the sea bottom.
There for a time we locked hands;
the sea churned with blood, and I severed the head
of Grendel's mother with a giant-sword
there in the war-hall; taxed to the limit, 2140
I made off with my life: death hadn't marked me;
and the kinsman of Healfdene, guardian of men,
once more gave me magnificent treasures.
    "So that king lived as custom demands;
I was not deprived of the promised reward 2145
my strength had earned me, the son of Healfdene
heaped these arms with radiant treasures—
these, lord, I will lay before you,
bestow with courtesy. As before, all depends
on your beneficence; I have few 2150
close kinsmen, Higelac, except you."

He commanded a boar insignia be carried in,
a helmet that had towered in battle, chain mail,
and a stately war-sword; then said these words:
2155 "Hrothgar gave me this war-gear,
the wise prince bade me say
first of all, he cherishes your friendship;
he said King Heorogar, leader of the Scyldings,
had it in his keeping a long time;
2160 nonetheless he would not leave the breast-guard
to his own son, the valiant Heoroweard,
loyal though he was. Use it well!"
I heard that four horses, identical bays
glossy as apples rapidly followed
2165 that treasure. He heaped gift on gift
of horse and harness. So should a kinsman act,
never weaving with secret cunning
treacherous nets, plotting death
for comrades in arms. To the valiant Higelac
2170 his nephew was entirely devoted
and each thought only of the other's comfort.
I heard he gave Hygd that same necklace,
gold studded with garnets, which Wealtheow
had granted him, together with three horses,
2175 supple and saddle-bright. After the ring-bequeathal
her breast was adorned with the golden torque.
    So Beowulf revealed himself brave;
martial in war and merciful in peace,
he sought glory. Nor did he slay
2180 his hearth-companions in drunken frenzy;
nor was he savage of temper: he reserved for battle
that peerless strength, prodigious gift
God had given him. He had been reckoned
a worthless boy; the Weders held
2185 he was weak-spirited, and the Weder lord
seldom thought of him at feast time.
They firmly believed he was slack in judgment,
slothful in bearing. Change, and that sudden,
came to the glorious man for each of his griefs.
2190   The protector of men, puissant in battle,
commanded Hrethel's gold-encrusted
heirloom be borne in. The Geats possessed
no other sword so jewel-luminous.
He laid it upon Beowulf's lap

and granted him an immense kingdom, 2195
throne and stronghold. Both ruled their lands
by ancestral right, bonded by blood
to their inheritance, though he whose birth
was higher held a greater realm.

It came to pass in later days 2200
after Higelac fell in the press of battle
and war-swords reached through the shield-wall
slaying Heardred, when the Battle Scylfings,
the blood-lust on them, singled him out
among his victorious soldiers, and struck him down, 2205
Hereric's nephew—that the broad kingdom
passed in time into Beowulf's hands.
He ruled it well for fifty winters,
an old man at the last, ancient land steward—
until one began by darkest night 2210
to usurp his power, hold sway in his place—
a dragon on the heath which guarded its hoard
under a high cairn. Unknown to men,
a path led there. Some fugitive from slaughter
discovered it by chance. He crept inside, 2215
and from the heathen hoard seized a cup,
a jewelled goblet. The dragon avenged that,
though sleeping he had been robbed by a thief's
sleight of hand. The folk in villages
neighboring the cave soon learned of its choler. 2220

   A reluctant thief had broached the wyrm-hoard,
arousing the dragon. Bitter necessity,
not free choice, drew him thither,
the servant of warriors who, outcast, had fled
vicious blows, and there reached inside 2225
that sin-troubled man . . . .
. . . .
. . . .
. . . .
. . . . 2230
. . . . Within the earth-hall
were a great many ancestral treasures,
a magnificent legacy of luminous things
which princes long ago in their fathomless thought
had laid by. Death had claimed them 2235

years ago, and he who remained
alone of that folk, who stirred there longest,
keeper in his grief of what his friends
no longer kept, knew this as well—
2240 soon, he, too, would have little use
for the hoarded treasure. A barrow was prepared
on the windy headland within earshot of the waves,
fashioned and made fast by daedalian craft.
The ring-keeper carried within
2245 noble treasure—gold cups and such utensils
as should be saved. He said these words:
"Hold thou, earth, now that men cannot,
the possessions of princes. They first plundered it
from you; war-death trundled them away,
2250 violent slaughter took each beloved
lord and kinsman who gave up this life,
joyed in fellowship. None have I
who bears a sword, or polishes the jewelled
drinking cup. My lords journeyed hence.
2255 So must the helmet braided with gold
be shorn of ornament; the polisher sleeps
who might have burnished the battle-mask
and, likewise, the armor which tasted at war
the bite of iron over the clashing of shields,
2260 moulders with the man. Nor can the ringed
corselet travel far from the clasp
of the fallen warrior. There is no harp-pleasure,
no joy of plucked wood, no hawk
to glide through the hall, nor swift horse
2265 to beat upon the cobbled yard. Cruel death
hath sent the mortal creatures forth!"
So grieving in spirit, he mourned his losses,
the disconsolate man paced the barrow
by day and night until resistless death
2270 lay hold of his heart. The ancient dawn-predator,
venomous dragon which, burning,
inhabits barrows and flies by night
shrouded in flame, found out the unguarded
glorious hoard; every earthdweller
2275 instinctively fears him. Compelled by nature,
he ferrets out hoards of heathen gold,
which he guards for centuries; it does him no good.
    For three hundred years, the man-ravager,

strong as a giant, kept watch in the earth
over the treasure-mound, until a man 2280
aroused its wrath; carried off a gold
cup to his prince, begged sanctuary
of his liege lord. The hoard was ransacked,
emptied of rings, the boon granted
the destitute man. For the first time 2285
the king set eyes on the brilliant heirlooms.
Then the wyrm awoke, the feud resumed;
the impetuous one sniffed along the wall,
caught scent of its foe. With great stealth
he had slipped by the coiled dragon. 2290
So may a man, if death has not marked him,
and he's faithful to God, pass unscathed
through flood and fire. The hoard's protector
combed the surroundings, sought the man
who'd dealt it such a blow while it slept. 2295
Burning with anger, it circled the barrow
again and again: but no man was there
in the empty waste—it was keen on slaughter,
eager to kill; then it rooted through the barrow,
searched for the treasure, and found in a moment 2300
someone had rifled its gold,
its precious possessions. The hoard's protector
had one desire—that the night come.
Bitterly angry, the barrow-keeper
longed to repay the loss of chalices 2305
with draughts of fire. Day speedily waned
as the wyrm willed; it did not linger
on the cliff but went forth in flame,
a gliding fire. The onset was dreadful
for the neighboring folk; all the more so 2310
since their ring-giver would soon come to grief.

    The intruder began to spew hot gleeds,
fire the bright houses. Those flaring rushlights
horrified men. The hostile flyer
would spare nothing that moved or breathed. 2315
Signs of the wyrm's wrath, its cruel
enmity, were branded deep in the landscape.
The war-scather harassed and humbled
the Geatish folk; before daybreak
it darted back to its gold-hall and hoard. 2320
It had enveloped in fire, in gouts of flame,

the neighboring peoples; it trusted its war-strength,
the walls of its barrow; that trust was betrayed.
    Soon to Beowulf the word was brought,
2325 the grim message that his own house,
loveliest of halls, had gone up in flames,
the Geats' gift-throne. To that good man
it was a piercing sorrow, the fiercest heart-grief.
He began to think that through some trespass
2330 (had he broken the old law?) Almighty God
was bitterly offended. Dark misgivings
obsessed him, as was not his wont.
The fire-drake had consumed in flame
the towering hall, the tribal stronghold
2335 on the sea-coast. The war-king of the Weders,
lord and protector of warrior and noble,
devised a revenge for his tormentor:
he commanded a shield of solid iron
be forged. He reckoned wood useless—
2340 a linden shield could not withstand
dragon-fire. Now must they both
endure the passage from their mortal days,
their life's limit, both prince and wyrm—
though it had held its hoarded wealth a long while.
2345 The ring-giver scorned the counsel
that he should bring the far-flyer to bay
with a large force. He did not fear the conflict
nor brood one moment on the wyrm's prowess,
its strength and courage: he'd been too often
2350 in dire straits, compassed by dangers
in the din of battle, since he had cleansed
Hrothgar's hall—the glory-hungry man—
and crushed at war Grendel's kinsfolk,
that cruel breed.
                  That was no common
2355 hand-combat where Higelac fell,
after the Weders' king, beloved lord,
Hrethel's son, in a brief skirmish
on Frisian shores drank his death-draught
from an iron sword. Beowulf survived
2360 through his own strength, endured the sea-trial—
on one arm alone he bore thirty
suits of armor when he stepped into the sea.
The Hetwars who opposed him

with lifted shields had no cause to boast
of the battle's outcome; few who fought 2365
with the warrior ever saw their homes again!
Alone and destitute, the son of Ecgtheow
labored over the sea to his homeland.
There Hygd tempted him with gold and a kingdom,
rings and a prince's throne; she feared her son 2370
could not defend the ancestral seat
from invading armies, now that Higelac was dead.
Yet the kingless people could not persuade him
by any means to assume the rule,
become Heardred's chosen lord; 2375
he refused every offer of royal power.
Instead he gave the prince a friend's counsel,
held him in honor and helped him to rule
until he came of age.
                         Ohthere's sons,
banished exiles, sought him out. 2380
They had been disloyal to the Scylfing leader,
most munificent of the sea-kings
who granted gifts in Swedish realms,
an illustrious lord. That meant his death—
the son of Higelac received a mortal wound, 2385
a sword thrust, for harboring them.
Heardred fallen, Ongentheow's son
again set forth to reach his home,
allowed Beowulf the prince's throne,
the rule of the Geats. He was a good king. 2390

  In later days, he found the means
to requite that regicide. He befriended Eadgils,
that destitute man, son of Ohthere,
furthered his cause with warriors and weapons
sent over the sea. Full payment came 2395
through his punitive raid: a king perished.
  So the son of Ecgtheow survived each peril,
faced vicious combat with radiant
courage until the day came to pass
when he must fight with the wyrm. 2400
Impatient with anger, the lord of the Weders
went, one of twelve, to view the dragon:
by now, he had learned how the feud arose,
the nightmare to men: the jewel-heavy chalice

2405 fell into his grasp from the talebearer's hand.
He was the thirteenth man among that troop,
he who earlier had unleashed the onslaught,
the grief-striken caitiff, the abject one,
who guided them. Against his will he went
2410 to where he alone knew the sunken hall,
barrow under the earth near the pounding sea,
the violent surf; it was heaped inside
with gems and braided gold. A monstrous guard—
able combatant—had kept the golden treasure
2415 time out of mind under the earth: no easy purchase
for the man avid of possessing it.
The battle-tempered king sat down on the headland;
the Geats' gold-friend bade his comrades
God-speed: his spirit was grieving,
2420 wavering like a flame and deathward bent:
doom was approaching to take the old one,
seize his soul-hoard, cut asunder
spirit from body: but a short time more
would the aetheling's soul be robed in flesh.
2425   Beowulf spoke, the son of Ecgtheow:
"Many skirmishes I survived in my youth,
in times of war; I summon them to mind.
I was seven when the gold-prince,
the folk's friend and lord, received me from my father;
2430 King Hrethel raised me and ruled me,
gave me jewels and drink, as befitted our kinship.
I was no less dear to him,
a young prince in his house, than any of his sons—
Herebeald, Haethcyn, or my Higelac.
2435 The eldest was laid in his deathclay
most unfairly through a kinsman's hand,
after Haethcyn with a horn-bow
let fly the shaft that struck his lord,
took aim in error and felled his kinsman,
2440 his own brother with a bloody arrow.
That was a wound not to be healed, gaping
in memory, chafing to the spirit; nonetheless,
the unavenged aetheling was severed from his life.
    "Likewise, it is sad for an old man
2445 to abide the hanging of his son
from the gallow's tree; then will he keen
to himself, croon words he knows not what

when the ravens sport with the swinging boy:
despite his years, he could do nothing.
Each dawn is bitter with the memory 2450
of his son's journey hence; he has no heart
to watch another grow to manhood,
claim his inheritance, when he has seen
what death will do to one so young.
In his grief he gazes on his son's house, 2455
the deserted hall, the draughty fire-place
where the wind is chattering—the horseman sleeps,
the soldier in his sepulchre; there is no stirring
of harp or hawk as there was before.
2460
   "He turns then to his bed, the one alone
sings a grief-song for the absent one—
all too spacious the plains and the dwelling places.
   "So the Weders' lord nursed a restless
sorrow for Herebeald, yet could find no means
because of that fratricide for settling the feud. 2465
His hands were tied: he could not persecute the warrior
for his cruel deeds, though he did not count him dear.
Borne down by that burden, the grief which had befallen him,
he withdrew from human things to worship God;
he left to his sons villages and lands, 2470
as a blessed man will, when he passed away.
   "Hostilities flared again between the Geats and Swedes
once Hrethel died; the sea linked them
in mutual enmity, armies skirmished
on newly scoured beaches: Ongentheow's sons, 2475
like ravening wolves, set no stock in peace,
but treacherous ambush became their obsession
as they fell on their prey near Slaughter Hill.
My friends and lords settled that account
of fierce misdeed as you have heard, 2480
though one paid for it with his heart's blood,
an exorbitant price: war proved
fatal to Haethcyn, the Geats' lord.
On the morrow the surviving kinsman
made good his revenge with the edge of a sword, 2485
when Ongentheow grappled with Eofor;
his war-helmet shattered, the ancient Scylfing
fell, corpse-pale; one hand remembered
abundant loss, and struck the death-blow.

2490	"I repaid him for the treasures he gave me
	by doing him service with this bright sword,
	as fate allowed; I owed him everything,
	houses and fields I possessed in joy.
	He had no need to recruit from the Gifthas,
2495	the Spear-Danes or Swedes, purchase mercenaries
	and they poor quality, at great expense.
	I had one wish: to go before him on foot,
	alone in front of them all, and so shall I
	do always at war, as long as this sword
2500	endures which has served me so often
	since I stood among the veterans in the thick of battle
	and slew Day-Raven, the Huga champion,
	by hand: he was helpless to carry homeward
	the jewelled brooch to the Frisian king.
2505	The standard bearer fell in battle,
	the aetheling in his courage, nor was a sword his slayer.
	A battle-grip stilled his heartbeat,
	crushed his ribcage. Now with cold steel,
	with hand and sword, shall I assay the treasure."
2510	Beowulf spoke, said vaunt-words
	for the final time: "I went on many campaigns
	in my youth; an aged king,
	I yet will take up arms, accomplish
	famous deeds, if the manslayer
2515	dare venture forth from out the earth-hall."
	Then he addressed each of the warriors,
	his loyal men, for the last time,
	the valiant one in his helmet: "I would carry no sword,
	no weapon against the wyrm, grapple in such wise
2520	with the monster as I did once with Grendel,
	if by such means I might keep my word;
	but I expect there a perilous fire,
	envenomed breath. Thus it is I bear
	both shield and corselet. I shall hold my ground
2525	against the barrow's lord: we both shall abide
	the ruling of fate, what the Measurer of every mortal
	has allotted us. Firm in my resolve,
	I shall forego all boasting about the winged predator.
	Await by the barrow, you warriors in harness,
2530	safe in your armor, the outcome of our contest—
	which of us two shall pass unscathed
	through mortal combat. That is not your concern,

nor is any man's strength sufficient, except mine,
to match the demon, blow for blow,
achieve glory. Either courage shall place 2535
the gold in my grasp, or war will take me,
and a violent death be your lord's."
   Arose then in his battle-harness,
the famous warrior, stern in visage,
under the rockface, trusting in the strength 2540
of one man; a coward does not act so!
He saw by the cliff—that one in all ways
courageous, who had survived the clashing
of armies on foot countless times—
a stone-arch standing, a stream bursting 2545
forth from the barrow; the torrent was veined
with gouts of fire: beyond lay the gold
down the chamber he could not broach
without burning in the dragon's breath.
When his rage had mounted beyond containment, 2550
he drew forth a challenge from deep in his chest,
the great-hearted one cried out; like struck bronze, his voice
came echoing under the grey stone.
The hoard-keeper heard the man's voice
incited to hatred; there was little time 2555
to parley a truce. In a moment came
a noxious breath, an acid vapor
from under the stone; the earth trembled.
Alone by the barrow, the lord of the Geats
turned his shield toward the fierce stranger. 2560
The coiled thing's heart was keen
on seeking battle. His sword was drawn,
the good war-king's precious heirloom,
thirsty blade; each to the other
death-minded one was horror incarnate. 2565
The resolute man, prince of warriors,
steadied his shield, when the wyrm coiled
swiftly together; he waited in his armor.
Then serpentlike, gliding in fires,
it rushed toward its judgment. Shield did its office, 2570
protected the great prince, his life and limbs,
for not so long as he might have wished,
where for the first time, he must hold his own
without hope—fate had not ordained him
triumph in battle. The lord of the Geats 2575

lifted his hand, struck the mottled carapace
with Ing's heirloom—to no effect, the luminous
blade glanced off bone, cut not so deeply
as its master, a people's king, had need,
2580 beset by torments. The barrow's warden
bridled with anger after that blow,
vomited a corpse-making flame; cruel fire
leaped through the chamber. The gold-friend of the Geats
said nothing about triumph. Unsheathed, his war-sword
2585 had failed him in combat, as it should not have,
virtuous iron. Nor was it a pleasant hour
when Ecgtheow's glorious kinsman must be stripped
of his mortal vestments and the earth itself;
against his will, he must find lodgings
2590 elsewhere, as each man must,
his tenure expired.
     It was not long
before the deadly combatants grappled again.
The hoard's warden took heart, its thorax filled
with a flood of breath; he who had ruled a kingdom
2595 was compassed by fire, and made helpless.
Comrades-at-arms, the seed of aethelings,
distinguished by valor, did not stand
in throngs at his side; they had taken to their heels
to save their skins. Of them, one alone
2600 was heavy at heart; nothing can blot kinship
from the memory of a man who weighs things rightly.

  He was Wiglaf, Weohstan's son,
kinsman to Aelfhere; a valued warrior,
man of the Scylfings; who beheld his own lord,
2605 his helmeted visage, seared by the heat.
He called to mind his generous gifts,
the lands and waters of the Waymundings,
ancestral rights his father possessed, now his.
He could not stand by; he seized his shield
2610 of yellow linden, his ancient sword
known among men as Eanmund's, son
of Ohthere's, heirloom; at battle it happened
Weohstan killed the friendless exile
with his own sword, and bore to his kinsman
2615 radiant spoils—helmet, chain mail,
and the sword of a giant; Onela granted him

his nephew's war-gear,
serviceable armor—and kept silent
about the killing though his brother-son lay dead.
He held on to them for many years,   2620
both sword and corselet, until his son
had proved equal in deed to that patrimony;
his was a vast legacy to his son—
abundant war-gear—when he set forth
on the final journey. For the first time   2625
the young champion must hazard his life
in a violent skirmish at his lord's side.
His heart did not quail, his kinsman's heirloom
betrayed no one, as the wyrm discovered
when they had met together in combat.   2630
    Wiglaf spoke, sick at heart,
said much to his comrades concerning their duty:
"I recall the time when we drank mead
and pledged to our lord, who gave us rings
in the fire-lit hall flowing with drink,   2635
that we would redeem his gifts to us,
both helmet and hard sword, should it happen
his need be such. From all his army
he chose us to do his bidding,
reckoned us worth a hero's wage   2640
because he judged us capable warriors,
valiant men-at-arms—yet our lord
planned to perform this courage-work
alone, because he, the keeper
of a kingdom, excels all men in glory   2645
and perilous deeds. Now the day is come
when our liege lord has need of the strength
of resolute warriors; let us go forth
to bolster the war-prince, as long as it lives,
the cruel fire-lizard! God knows this: 2650
I would much rather my own body
be shrouded in flame with my gold-friend.
It would do us dishonor to bear these shields
back to our dwellings, unless we first
fell the dragon, defend the life   2655
of the Weders' lord. It's a hard thing,
and poor payment for his ancient sacrifice
that he alone must suffer pain,
humbled in battle. Both sword and helmet,

2660 corselet and battle-cloak, we will share like brothers."
Through the deadly smoke he went in his war-helmet
to serve his lord, said these few words:
"Dear Beowulf, you've acquitted yourself well,
remaining true to your youthful promise
2665 that so long as you lived you would never let
your glory be eclipsed. Now, my resolute prince,
you must summon your courage and all your strength
to defend your life; I will help you."
    After these words, the wyrm in its ire
2670 struck a second time, the cruel visitant
crested in flame, killer of men,
closed in on its foes. Surging fire consumed
the shield to its rim, the corselet could not
perform its office for the young warrior;
2675 nonetheless, the youth in his courage took refuge
under his kinsman's shield, when his own
was swallowed in flame. A remembrance of glory
stirred the war-king, vast in his strength,
he struck with his blade, so it shivered against
2680 the monster's skull: Naegling splintered,
Beowulf's ancient, grey-hued sword
failed in combat. It was not fated
the iron blade could assist him
in battle. That hand was too strong,
2685 as I have heard, it shattered every blade
he bore into combat, overtaxing wound-
quenched metal; it profited him not.
    For the third time, the cruel fire-drake,
the scourge of nations, was ready to strike—
2690 billowing with flame, it rushed them
at the first chance; sharp fangs
dug at his neck, drew blood,
living substance welled from the wound.

    Then, as I have heard, at his sovereign's need,
2695 the warrior revealed his native courage,
the strength and spirit he held as birthright.
He did not aim at its head, yet fire singed off
the valiant's hand when he helped his kinsman,
and he struck the dragon lower down,
2700 the man in his armor, burying the sword
hilt-deep so that afterwards the fire

began to sink. Then the king himself
acted quickly, drew forth the sleek dagger,
blood-quenched and bitter, he carried at his belt;
the Weders' lord cut deep into the wyrm. 2705
They killed the enemy, extinguished its life;
by their courage, the kinsmen, acting as one,
worked its doom. So should men do
when there is need. That was the king's
final victory, his hands' last 2710
work in this world.
     The wound the earth-drake
inflicted on him began to swelter
and swell; in a short while he felt
the poison working inwards, the fatal
venom in his breast. The aetheling went then, 2715
found a ledge by the wall where he sat,
the deep-minded one; he gazed on the giants' masonry—
arches of stone and the columns locking them
eternally in place within the earth-hall.
Then, with blood-soaked hands, the most excellent thane 2720
washed the wounds of his liege lord,
gently attended the glorious prince
sated with war, and unfastened his helmet.
 Beowulf spoke in spite of his wounds,
the mortal dragon-marks; he knew beyond a doubt 2725
he had come to the end of his allotted span,
his earthly joys; the measure of his days
was vanishing away, sifting toward death:
"Now would I give to my own son
these war-gear had it been ordained 2730
that any heir, flesh of my flesh,
survived me. I ruled my people
fifty winters. There was not a king,
not one of those encircling our borders,
who dared send warriors against me, 2735
threatened hostility. I awaited in my realm
the fate shaped for me, bore myself well,
nor took part in treachery, nor swore
false oaths. In all this, I can
exult, despite my mortal wounds. 2740
Therefore, the Lord of Life cannot reproach me
for the slaughter of kinsmen when the breath is winnowed
from my body. Go swiftly,

dear Wiglaf, and examine the hoard
2745 under the grey stone, now that the wyrm lies still,
sorely wounded in its treasureless sleep.
Hasten on your errand so I may see the storied
wealth, and gaze on braided gold,
radiant jewel-work, and with that glimpse
2750 of magnificent wealth relinquish more gently
the life and lordship which I long held."

Then, as I have heard, the son of Weohstan—
as soon as the wounded prince had finished the speech—
obeyed his broken king, went in chain mail—
2755 woven battle-shirt—under the barrow's roof.
Once he had passed inside, the brave young kinsman—
victorious thane—saw the cold glister
of gold and jewels along the ground,
phosphorescence on the walls, and in the den itself
2760 of the ancient dawn-floater, cups standing,
chalices of vanished tribes, their ornaments eaten away,
and no one to polish them; there were many a helm,
old and rust-bitten, unnumbered bracelets
woven with cunning. Stones and gold
2765 within the earth may easily betray
the human heart, hide them who will!
And he saw hanging there a golden standard,
high above the hoard, the greatest of hand-works,
woven by skilled fingers; from it, light shone,
2770 allowing him to study the expanse of the floor,
the gathered artifacts. Of the wyrm, no trace
remained: the blade had taken it.
Then, as I have heard, he plundered the hoard,
rifled the work of ancient gold-smiths,
2775 scooped chalice and plate into his arms,
all that he wanted; snatched also the standard,
loveliest of banners. An iron blade
had put to sleep the zealous sentinel,
the ancient protector, avid of gold,
2780 who had kept vigil, greeted trespassers
with torrents of fire, night-billowing
venomous flame, until death put it out.
He went in haste, eager to return,
(the gold was beautiful); and he had to know
2785 if the valiant one, the mortally wounded

lord of the Weders, yet lived
on that patch of clay where he'd taken his leave.
Burdened with treasure, breathless, he found
the glorious prince soaked in blood,
his life at an end; again he sprinkled   2790
water on him, until words pierced
his spirit's reticence.
                  The hero-king spoke,
old in grief, he contemplated the gold:
"Now must I praise the Maker for this,
thank Him, the Giver of Glory, Lord   2795
of Light, that I look upon these jewels,
grateful I had the strength to win them
for my people before my death-day.
Since I have purchased the treasure-hoard
with the life left me, you must take care   2800
of our tribe henceforth; I can stay no longer.
Call upon the courageous to heap a mound
and light a bonfire on the sea-beaten cliff;
it shall tower high on Whale's Head
as a remembrance to my people,   2805
so that afterwards seafarers will name it
Beowulf's Barrow—they who pilot
their ships far on the darkening flood."
The valiant king unclasped from his neck
a golden collar, gave to his thane,   2810
the young warrior, his helm of hammered
gold, ring and corselet; bade that he use them well:
"You are the last living remnant of our line,
the Waymundings; wyrd has swept them off,
all my kinsmen, each prince in his courage,   2815
to be winnowed as the Lord will. I must follow them."
That was the last utterance of the old one's
pondering heart before death assayed him,
the singeing fires; the soul flew
from his breast, seeking righteous judgment.   2820

   Now the young man must suffer the pain
of seeing the one he held most dear
drink the last bitter lees
of a hard death. His killer also lay
robbed of life, the viperish dragon   2825
slaughtered outright. The coiling wyrm

could no longer keep its ring-hoard—
the iron blade had claimed it, the leaving
of hammers steeped in battle—
2830 now the wide-flyer, stilled by wounds,
lay on the earth near the treasure-hall.
It did not wheel upon the wind anymore,
exulting in treasure, blazing forth
by pitch-black night: one warrior's
2835 capable hand had dragged it to earth.
Indeed, I have heard of few men,
however strong and bold in spirit,
whom it might speed to venture against the breath
of that venomous monster or touch and so disturb
2840 the repose of things within that ring-hall—
if they found the warder waking
who dwells in the barrow. For Beowulf
death was the payment for his portion of treasure;
both man and dragon had come to the end
2845 of their loaned lives.
     Before long,
those who had fled the battle left the wood,
ten all told of the abject oath-breakers,
who had lacked the heart to lift their spears
in their lord's great need;
2850 dragging their shields, hangdog in their shame,
they went in their dishonor to where the old one lay;
stared on Wiglaf. Exhausted, he sat there,
the loyal foot-soldier by his lord's side,
and laved him with water; it was too late.
2855 He hadn't the power, despite his fierce desire,
to sustain life in the ancient prince,
or turn aside the Ruler's will;
His judgment held sway over the acts
of every man, as it still does.
2860 Scathing words for those who'd forfeited their courage
came readily enough to the young man's lips.
Wiglaf, the son of Weohstan, spoke,
the heart-broken man looked upon the dishonored:
 "He who values truth can justly say
2865 that the lord who granted you treasure,
gave you the war-dress which you yet wear—
when he bestowed helmet and mail-coat
to his men-at-arms gathered in the mead-hall—

the most splendid equipage a prince could give 2870
and a soldier receive in any dominion—
I say that lord threw helmet and sword
away, wasted gold as if it were dirt.
Our king had little reason to boast
of his comrades at war; nonetheless the Lord God, 2875
Wielder of Victories, allowed him vengeance,
alone with his sword, when he had need of courage.
I had but feeble means to shield
his life at battle, and so I strived
beyond my power to help my kinsman. 2880
I struck repeatedly with my sword,
and the venomous thing weakened, fire streamed
less fiercely from its mouth. Yet few were the defenders
thronging the prince in his great peril.
Now your kindred shall forego all ceremony— 2885
the granting of sword and cup relinquish,
all hope of joy; each man of your line
shall forfeit his title to inherited lands
when the extent of your cowardice—
the dishonor of your deeds—is fully revealed
to high-ranking men. A true warrior 2890
prefers death to a life of disgrace."

    He ordered them to announce the battle's outcome
above the cliff-edge, where the shield-bearers,
the high-born of the tribe, had sat the long morning
grieving and thinking on the uncertain issue— 2895
would the dear man meet death this day
or return again? The horseman on the cliff
kept silent but a short time
before telling them the message he bore:
"Now is our source of joy, our gold- 2900
granting lord fast in his death bed,
slaughter-cold he sleeps, through the work of the wyrm;
beside him lies his mortal enemy
weakened by dagger-wounds; alone, his sword
proved impotent against the monster, 2905
and could not wound it. Wiglaf, the son
of Weohstan, sits by Beowulf,
the living warrior beside the dead;
grieving, he keeps corpse-watch
over the dear and the despised. 2910

"Now a prospect of war
awaits our people, once our king's fall
is common knowledge among the Frisians
and Franks. The feud with the Hugas grew
bitter after Higelac ventured by ship
2915 to the Frisian shore: that violent tribe
engaged him in combat, and pressed its advantage
with a stronger force, sweeping the field,
and so he fell, the mailed warrior
was cut down and killed. That day the prince
2920 gave no rings to his retainers. Since then,
little love has been lost between us.

"Nor do I look for peace from the Swedes,
or anything but treachery, given our past contentions—
because Ongentheow slew Haethcyn,
2925 Hrethel's son, near Raven's Wood,
when the Weders, in excess of pride,
sought war with the Scylfings.
The ancient father of Ohthere—implacable
as he was old—struck back with his sword—
2930 cut down the sea-king, rescued his wife,
the ancient crone robbed of her gold,
mother of Onela and Ohthere;
and harried forth his sworn enemies
who, leaderless now, ran headlong
2935 to the dubious refuge of Raven's Wood.
He encircled the wounded survivors
with a vast encampment; all night long
he taunted the wretched men with torture—
said he'd take them and flay them
2940 with naked steel, strung up in trees
as sport for crows. With dawn came comfort
for the discouraged men: Higelac's horn
rang through the joyless wood; they heard
his brazen trumpet, when the great one came,
2945 following their tracks with his chosen men.

"The slaughter path was plainly manifest—
the Swedes and Weders had struggled bitterly
and the gaping corpses all but said so.
Ongentheow marshalled his forces,
2950 solemn now and grieving, he sought his stronghold,
retreated with his men to a safe position;

he had heard of Higelac's prowess,
the war-strength of the proud one; he did not trust
his power to repel the sea-men,
defend his treasure, his wife and sons, 2955
from the hostile invaders; again he fell back,
gasping under the battlements. Now the Geats harried
the Swedish soldiery, Higelac's banner
was borne in triumph over the enemy's threshold,
as the Hrethelings overran their position. 2960
Then it was that white-haired Ongentheow
was brought to bay at sword-point—
king though he was, he must submit
to Eofor's judgment. Angrily,
Wulf—Wonred's son—struck with his sword, 2965
a clean blow that spattered the blood
from scalp-veins. Even so, the old Scylfing
did not flinch, but speedily repaid
that slaughter blow with a fiercer remittance,
when the folk-king wheeled to face him. 2970
Nor could the valiant son of Wonred
match the old man blow for blow—
he was struck on the skull, his helmet shorn—
covered in blood, he doubled over,
fell to his knees. He was not yet fey, 2975
he regained his strength, though sorely wounded.
His brother fallen, Higelac's vigilant thane
swung his broadsword across the shield-wall,
battered the other's helmet with a blade
once wielded by giants; then fell the king, 2980
the folk's shepherd, severed from life.
Many were the men who bandaged their comrades,
helped them to their feet between battle surges
to claim victory in that place of carnage.
Then man stripped man of his gear, 2985
tore from Ongentheow his iron coat,
his jewelled helmet and his sword also;
bore to Higelac the old man's armor.
He received the treasure and sweetly promised
fitting recompense, and so fulfilled his pledge. 2990
When Eofor and Wulf arrived home,
the lord of the Weders, Hrethel's son,
rewarded their combat with a more than liberal hand,
gave each of them a king's ransom

2995 in lands and braided gold—no man on Middle-Earth
need gainsay that gift, such was their glory;
and crowned it all by granting Eofor
his sole daughter, hearth's adornment, as wife in wedlock.
　　"Because of this feuding and fierce hatred,
3000 this unburied blood-lust we can expect
a prompt incursion from the Swedish people,
once they learn that our lord is lifeless,
he who before held sceptre and hoard
against all threats, after the fall of warriors,
3005 the brave shield-bearers, and brought comfort
to our people, saved us more than once
through his noble labors. Now must we go
attend our king a final time,
bear him who gave us braided gold
3010 to his burning place. No small tribute
shall perish with our prince, but there is heaped
countless treasures dearly bought
and now, at the last, these rings he purchased
with his own life. Let flame take them,
3015 ravenous fire—no man shall covet
these treasures in his heart, nor shining woman
wear this gold-work at her throat,
but bent and grieving, stripped of adornment,
they will pass as exiles into a far country,
3020 now that the war-prince has laid laughter aside,
and every pleasure. Henceforth the spear
shall be seized in the chill of dawn,
hands will close on cold metal; harp music
shall not wake the warrior, but the black raven
3025 over the soon-to-die shall caw merrily,
and say to the eagle the feast he had
when he and the wolf gorged on corpses."
　　So the valiant man foretold
the approaching peril; he deceived them
3030 on few counts. The company stood up,
crept joylessly under Eagle-Head,
beheld the wonder with tear-dimmed eyes.
There they found him soulless on the sand,
rigid in his last sleep—he who had granted rings
3035 but a short time before; the final day
had come for the war-king, the Weders' lord
had met with an unexpected death.

Yet first they saw a stranger creature—
the wyrm lying hard by its slayer
there on the beach, the fire-drake   3040
appallingly blotched, and blistered by gleeds;
fifty feet in length it measured
from snout to tail. It had joyed in flight,
and passed like a brand thrown into darkness,
to retire at dawn; death gripped it now: 3045
in the end it had found fitting use for the cave.
By them were strewn huge bowls and chalices,
sword-hilts heavy with garnets,
all eaten by rust, as they had lain
a thousand winters wasting in the earth.   3050
The heirlooms were possessed of a deep enchantment,
charms had been worked into their gold
so none of humankind could reach into
that ring-hall, unless God Himself,
the King of Victories, permitted him—   3055
He is the Protector of men—His chosen creature,
to open the hoard, as He deemed right.

    It had gained nothing from all its greed—
that busy creature that had heaped and hidden
gold in its barrow. It had just slain   3060
one of a handful, and met, in turn,
a bitter revenge. It remains a mystery
how a great-hearted man will fare at the last
of his allotted span, when he can stay no longer,
feasting with his kinsmen in the mead-hall.   3065
So it was for Beowulf, who assayed the brutal cunning
of the barrow-keeper; he could not foretell
the wound that would sever him from the world.
Famous princes had laid a heavy curse
on cup and sword until Judgment Day,   3070
causing any man who plundered that place
to be plunged into sin, and cast among devils,
chained in hell and tormented for all eternity,
unless the gold-hungry man had been glanced by grace,
the favor of Him who possesses all.   3075
    Wiglaf spoke, the son of Weohstan:
"It often happens that many must suffer
for one man's will—so with us.
We could not convince our dear lord,

3080   shepherd of a kingdom, through any counsel
to abstain from combat with the gold-keeper,
let it remain sleeping, as it had for ages,
dwelling in darkness until the world's end.
He held to his appointed course; there is the hoard
3085   bitterly bought. No earthly power
could have robbed him of that destiny.
I was in there, I stood gaping
at gold beyond saying, when we had cleared a path—
for we met with no gentle reception
3090   under the earthwall. Hurriedly I seized
all I could lay hold of, a royal burden
of hoarded treasure, and hastened back
to my king. I found him still alive,
conscious and alert; in his pain he spoke
3095   of many matters and bade me address you:
asked that you build, as you were his friends,
a tall barrow at his burning-place—
and make it magnificent, a memorial in keeping
with his great stature as man and warrior—
3100   without rival on this earth for as long as he ruled.
Let us hasten on another journey,
to look upon this glittering gold-heap,
this wonder come to light. I will lead you
that you may feast your eyes, and gaze your fill
3105   on brooches and braided gold. Prepare the bier,
ready it swiftly against our return,
for then we will carry our king's body,
our precious friend, where long he shall
remain in the Lord's keeping."
3110   The son of Weohstan, proven in war,
bade them announce to land-holders
that men of property fetch from afar
timbers for the fire, and so bear them
to where the good man lay: "Now shall the hot gleed—
3115   dark-blossoming fire—devour the strength of a people,
that prince who oft survived showering steel
when the arrow-tempests unleashed in vengeance
broke over the shield-wall, and the shaft struck home,
the humming arrow, fledged like a hawk."
3120   Now the wise son of Weohstan
summoned from the host seven all told
of the king's thanes, the finest soldiers,

and descended with them into the close and dragon-
reeking darkness; he who led them
carried a brand of burning pitch. 3125
No lots were drawn for plundering the hoard
once the men saw how all of it lay
wasting in the hall, golden heirlooms
now guardianless; they had no qualms
about handling the treasure and hauling it out 3130
into broad daylight; and they shoved the dragon
over the cliff-edge, for the waves to swallow,
the flood to enfold the gold-keeper.
Then woven gold was loaded on a wagon,
countless objects, and the king with them, 3135
the ancient warrior, borne to Whale's Head.

    The men of the Geats gathered the timbers
and heaped them into a stately pyre,
stacking it high with helmets and shields,
bright coats of chain mail, as he had bade. 3140
Then they laid him in its midst, those men in mourning—
their own dear lord, their famous prince.
They ignited the dry wood, kindled
that greatest of corpse-fires; woodsmoke rose
black over the bonfire, the branching flames 3145
enwound with weeping—a gust came
and went—his bonehouse was broken open,
his heat-seared breast. With mourning hearts
they murmured their loss, their lord's death;
and an old woman with her hair bound-up 3150
sang a lament for Beowulf,
grief-crazed she spoke at length
of the evil in store for them all—
she foresaw a field of corpses and men with spears
harvesting the survivors. Heaven swallowed the smoke. 3155
    Then the Weders raised up a tower
at the cliff-edge, built it lofty and strong,
visible from afar by sailors at sea,
and in ten days the work was done,
the warrior's monument, and the wall engirding 3160
the remnant coals. So it was fashioned
with all the splendor human craft can attain.
Into the barrow went jewel and ring,
all of the armor which the violent men

3165 had rifled from the hoard a short time before;
they gave the treasure for the earth to keep,
gold to commingle with dirt, and there it lies
as useless to men as it was before.
Then valiant horsemen, the scion of princes,
3170 twelve of his thanes, rode about the tower.
Now would they lament and remember their king,
breaking into song to speak their loss;
they celebrated his greatness as a man, the unstained
quality of his courage, as it is fitting
3175 for men to praise and say aloud
their love for their lord when he goes forth,
sundered from them, and from his body, by death.
And so they lamented their king's fall—
those horsemen who had received gold from his hand.
3180 They said that of earthly kings
he was the sweetest in bearing, and the kindest of men,
the most courteous to his people, and the most eager for fame.

Selected Sources

Adams, Valerie. *An Introduction to Modern English Word-Formation*. London: Longman Group, 1973.

Alexander, Michael, trans. *Beowulf*. Harmondsworth: Penguin Books, 1973.

Almgren, Bertil, et al. *The Viking*. Gothenberg: Nordbok, 1976.

Andersson, Theodore M. "Tradition and Design in *Beowulf*." In *Old English Literature in Context: Ten Essays*, edited by John D. Niles, 90–106. Bury St. Edmunds: St. Edmundsbury Press, 1980.

Andrews, S. O. *Postscripts on Beowulf*. New York: Russell and Russell, 1969.

Apter, Ronnie. *Digging for the Treasure: Translation after Pound*. New York: Peter Lang, 1984. Reprint. New York: Paragon House, 1987.

Baird, Joseph L. "Unferth the Ðyle. *Medium Ævum* 39 (1970): 1–12.

Barley, Nigel F. "Old English Colour Classification: Where Do Matters Stand?" In *Anglo-Saxon England 3*, edited by Peter Clemoes, 15–28. Cambridge: University Press, 1974.

Bartlett, Adeline Courtney. *The Larger Rhetorical Patterns in Anglo-Saxon Poetry*. New York: Columbia University Press, 1935.

Batchelor, C. C. "The Style of the *Beowulf:* A Study of the Composition of the Poem." *Speculum* 12 (1937): 330–42.

Bateson, F. W. *English Poetry and the English Language*. Oxford: Clarendon Press, 1973.

Baugh, Albert C., and Thomas Cable. *A History of the English Language*. Englewood Cliffs, N.J.: Prentice-Hall, 1963.

Belitt, Ben. *Adam's Dream*. New York: Grove Press, 1978.

Benjamin, Walter. "The Task of the Translator." Translated by James Hynd and E. M. Valk. *Delos* 2 (1968): 76–99.

Benson, Larry D. "The Pagan Coloring in *Beowulf*." In *Old English Poetry: Fifteen Essays*, edited by Robert Creed, 193–213. Providence: Brown University Press, 1967.

Bessinger, J.B., ed. *A Concordance to the Anglo-Saxon Poetic Records*. London: Cornell University Press, 1978.

———. *A Short Dictionary of Anglo-Saxon Poetry in a Normalized Early West Saxon Orthography*. Toronto: University of Toronto Press, 1960.

———. "The Sutton Hoo Harp Replica and Old English Musical Verse." In *Old English Poetry: Fifteen Essays*, edited by Robert Creed, 3–26. Providence: Brown University Press, 1967.

Blake, Norman. *The English Language in Medieval Literature*. London: J. M. Dent and Son, 1977.

Bliss, A. J. "The Appreciation of Old English Metre." In *English and Medieval*

Studies: Presented to J. R. R. Tolkien on the Occasion of his Seventieth Birthday, edited by Norman Davis and Charles L. Wrenn, 27–40. London: Unwin Brothers, 1962.

Blomfield, Joan. "The Style and Structure of *Beowulf*." *Review of English Studies* 14 (1938): 396–403.

Bloomfield, Morton. "Understanding Old English Poetry." In *Essays and Explorations*, 59–82. Cambridge: Harvard University Press, 1970.

Bone, Gavin. *Anglo-Saxon Poetry: An Essay with Specimen Translations in Verse.* Oxford: Clarendon Press, 1943.

Bonjour, Adrien. *The Digressions in Beowulf. Medium Ævum* Monographs, no. 5. Oxford: Basil Blackwell, 1950.

———. *Twelve Beowulf Papers: 1940–1960.* Geneva: University of Neuchatel Press, 1962.

Bosworth, J. and T. N. Toller. *An Anglo-Saxon Dictionary.* Oxford: Clarendon Press, 1882–98.

Bracher, Frederick. "Understatement in Old English Poetry." *PMLA* 52 (1937): 915–34.

Brady, Caroline. "The Old English Nominal Compounds in '-rad." *PMLA* 67 (1952): 538–71.

———. "'Weapons' in *Beowulf*: An Analysis of the Nominal Compounds and an Evaluation of the Poet's Use of Them." In *Anglo-Saxon England 8*, edited by Peter Clemoes, 79–141. Cambridge: University Press, 1979.

Brodeur, Arthur Gilchrist. *The Art of Beowulf.* Berkeley: University of California Press, 1959.

Bronsted, Johannes. *The Vikings.* Translated by Kalle Skov. Harmondsworth: Penguin Books, 1973.

Bruce-Mitford, Rupert. *Aspects of Anglo Saxon-Archaeology.* London: Victor Gollancz, 1974.

Burchfield, R. W. "The Prosodic Terminology of Anglo-Saxon Scholars." In *Old English Studies in Honour of John C. Pope*, edited by Robert B. Burlin and Edward B. Irving, Jr., 171–202. Toronto: University of Toronto Press, 1974.

Burlin, Robert E. "Gnomic Indirection in *Beowulf*." In *Anglo-Saxon Poetry: Essays in Appreciation (for John McGalliard)*, edited by Lewis E. Nicholson and Dolores W. Frese, 141–49. Notre Dame, Ind.: University of Notre Dame Press, 1975.

———. "Inner Weather and Interlace." In *Old English Studies in Honour of John C. Pope*, edited by Robert Burlin and Edward Irving, Jr., 81–89. Toronto: University of Toronto Press, 1974.

Cable, Thomas. *The Meter and Melody of Beowulf.* London: University of Illinois Press, 1974.

Campbell, Alistair. "The Old English Epic Style." In *English and Medieval Studies: Presented to J. R. R. Tolkien on the Occasion of his Seventieth Birthday*, edited by Norman Davis and Charles L. Wrenn, 13–26. London: Allen and Unwin Ltd., 1962.

———. "The Use in *Beowulf* of Earlier Heroic Verse." In *England Before the Conquest*, edited by Peter Clemoes and Kathleen Hughes, 283–92. Cambridge: University Press, 1971.

Carrigan, Eamon. "Structure and Thematic Development in *Beowulf*." *Proceedings of the Royal Irish Academy* 66 (1967): 1–51.

Selected Sources 173

Chickering, Howell D., trans. *Beowulf*. Garden City, N.Y.: Anchor Press, 1977.

Cleasby, Richard, Gudbrand Vigfusson, and Sir William Craigie. *An Icelandic-English Dictionary*. 2d ed. Oxford: Clarendon Press, 1975.

Clemoes, Peter, "Action in *Beowulf* and Our Perception of It." In *Old English Poetry: Essays on Style*, edited by Daniel Calder, 147–68. Berkeley: University of California Press, 1979.

———. *Rhythm and Cosmic Order in Old English Christian Literature*. Cambridge: University Press, 1970.

Clover, Carol T. "The Germanic Context of the Unferth Episode." *Speculum* 55 (1980): 444–68.

The Compact Edition of the Oxford English Dictionary. New York: Oxford University Press, 1974.

Coomaraswamy, Ananda K. *Christian and Oriental Philosophy of Art*. New York: Dover Publications, 1956.

Cramp, Rosemary. "Beowulf and Archaeology." *Medieval Archaeology* 1 (1957): 57–77.

Creed, Robert. "The Making of an Anglo-Saxon Poem." *Journal of English Literary History* 26 (1959): 445–54.

Crossley-Holland, Kevin, trans. *Beowulf*. Cambridge: D. S. Brewer, 1977.

———, trans. *Storm*. New York: Farrar, Straus, and Giroux, 1970.

Dacey, Philip and David Jauss, eds. *Strong Measures: Contemporary American Poetry in Traditional Forms*. New York: Harper and Row, 1986.

Daunt, Marjorie. "Old English Verse and English Speech Rhythm." In *Essential Articles for the Study of Old English*, edited by Jess B. Bessinger, Jr. and Stanley J. Kahrl, 289–304. Hamden, Conn.: Archon Books, 1968.

———. "Some Modes of Anglo-Saxon Meaning." In *Memory of J. R. Firth*, edited by Bazell, Catford, Halliday, and Robins, 66–78. London: Longmans, Green, 1966.

Davidson, H. R. Ellis. *The Sword in Anglo-Saxon England*. Oxford: Clarendon Press, 1962.

Davie, Donald. *Purity of Diction in English Verse*. London: Chatto and Windus, 1952.

Derolez, Rene L. M. "'—And That Difficult Word, Garsecg' (Gummere)." *Modern Language Quarterly* 7 (1946): 445–52.

Donaldson, E. Talbot, trans. *Beowulf*. Edited by Joseph F. Tuso. New York: W. W. Norton, 1975.

Dobbie, Elliott van Kirk, ed. *Beowulf and Judith*. The Anglo-Saxon Poetic Records, no. 4. New York: Columbia University Press, 1953.

Dryden, John. *The Works of John Dryden*. Edited by Edward Niles Hooker and H. T. Swedenberg, Jr. Vol. 1. Berkeley: University of California Press, 1956.

Eberhart, Richard. *Collected Poems*. New York: Oxford University Press, 1976.

Eliason, Norman E. "Beowulf, Wiglaf, and the Wægmundings." In *Anglo-Saxon England* 7, edited by Peter Clemoes, 95–106. Cambridge: University Press, 1975.

———. "The Ðyle and Scop in *Beowulf*." *Speculum* 38 (1963): 267–84.

Eliot, T. S. *The Complete Poems and Plays*. New York: Harcourt, Brace, and World, 1962.

Fakudiny, Lydia. "The Art of Old English Verse Composition." *Review of English Studies* 21 (1970): 129–42, 257–66.

Fitts, Dudley. "The Poetic Nuance." In *On Translation*, edited by Reuben Brower, 32–47. Cambridge: Harvard University Press, 1959.

Frank, Roberta. *Old Norse Court Poetry: The Drottvætt Stanza*. Ithaca: Cornell University Press, 1978.

Fraser, G. S. *Metre, Rhyme, and Free Verse*. London: Methuen, 1970.

Frey, Charles. "Lyric in Epic: Hrothgar's Depiction of the Haunted Mere." *English Studies* 58 (1977): 296–303.

Friebert, Stuart and David Young, eds. *A Field Guide to Contemporary Poetry and Poetics*. New York: Longman, 1980.

Fry, Donald K., ed. *Finnsburh Fragment and Episode*. London: Methuen, 1974.

Garnett, James M., trans. *Beowulf: An Anglo-Saxon Poem, and the Fight at Finnsburg*. 2d ed. Boston: Ginn, 1895.

Gray, Thomas. *The Correspondence of Thomas Gray*. Edited by Paget Toynbee and Leonard Whibley. Vol. 1. Oxford: Clarendon Press, 1935.

Green, Charles. *Sutton Hoo*. London: Merlin Press, 1963.

Greenfield, Stanley B. and Fred C. Robinson, eds. *A Bibliography of Publications on Old English Literature to the End of 1972*. Toronto: University of Toronto Press, 1980.

Greenfield, Stanley B. "Esthetics and Meaning and the Translation of Old English Poetry." In *Old English Poetry: Essays on Style*, edited by Daniel G. Calder, 91–110. Berkeley: University of California Press, 1979.

―――. "The Formulaic Expression of the Theme of 'Exile' in Anglo-Saxon Poetry." *Speculum* 30 (1955): 200–206.

―――. "Grendel's Approach to Heorot: Syntax and Poetry." In *Old English Poetry: Fifteen Essays*, edited by Robert Creed, 275–84. Providence: Brown University Press, 1967.

―――. *The Interpretation of Old English Poems*. Boston: Routledge and Kegan Paul, 1972.

―――. "Syntactic Analysis and Old English Poetry." *Neuphilologische Mitteilungen* 64 (1963): 373–78.

―――, trans. *A Readable Beowulf*. Carbondale: Southern Illinois University Press, 1982.

Gross, Harvey. *Sound and Form in Modern Poetry*. Ann Arbor: University of Michigan Press, 1973.

Gummere, Francis B. "The Translation of *Beowulf*, and the Relations of Ancient and Modern English Verse." *American Journal of Philology* 7 (1886): 46–78.

Hachman, Rolf. *The Germanic Peoples*. Translated by James Hogarth. Geneva: Nagel Publishers, 1971.

Hall, John R. Clark. *A Concise Anglo-Saxon Dictionary*. 4th ed. Cambridge: University Press, 1975.

Hamer, Richard, trans. *A Choice of Anglo-Saxon Verse*. London: Faber and Faber, 1970.

Hansen, Elaine Tuttle. "Hrothgar's 'Sermon' in *Beowulf* as Parental Wisdom." In *Anglo-Saxon England* 10, edited by Peter Clemoes, 53–67. Cambridge: University Press, 1982.

Hardy, Adelaide. "The Christian Hero Beowulf and Unferð Ðyle." *Neophilologus* 53 (1969): 55–69.

Hart, Thomas. "Ellen: Some Tectonic Relationships in *Beowulf* and Their Formal Resemblance to Anglo-Saxon Art." *Papers on Language and Literature* 6 (1970): 263–90.

Hart, Walter Morris. *Ballad and Epic: A Study in the Development of the Narrative Art.* Harvard University Studies and Notes in Philology and Literature, vol. 11. Boston: Ginn, 1907.

Henderson, George. *Early Medieval.* Harmondsworth: Penguin Books, 1972.

Hopkins, Gerard Manley. *Poems and Prose of Gerard Manley Hopkins.* Edited by W. H. Gardner. Harmondsworth: Penguin Books, 1975.

Irving, Edward B. *A Reading of Beowulf.* New Haven: Yale University Press, 1968.

Jones, Gwyn. *A History of the Vikings.* Forge Village: Murray Printing Company for the Oxford University Press, 1968.

Kennedy, Charles, trans. *Beowulf.* New York: Oxford University Press, 1940.

Ker, W. P. *Epic and Romance: Essays in Medieval Literature.* London: MacMillan, 1908. Reprint. New York: Dover, 1957.

Klaeber, Fr., ed. *Beowulf.* 3d ed. Lexington, Mass.: D.C. Heath, 1950.

Lawrence, W. W. *Beowulf and Epic Tradition.* Cambridge: Harvard University Press, 1928.

Leech, Geoffrey. *A Linguistic Guide to English Poetry.* London: Longmans, Green, 1969.

Leonard, William Ellery, trans. *Beowulf.* New York: Heritage Club, 1939.

Leslie, Roy F. "Analysis of Stylistic Devices and Effects in Anglo-Saxon Literature." In *Stil- und Formprobleme in der Literatur*, edited by Paul Bockman, 129–36. Heidelberg: Carl Winter Universitätsverlag, 1959.

———. "The Editing of Old English Poetic Texts: Questions of Style." In *Old English Poetry: Essays on Style*, edited by Daniel Calder, 111–25. Berkeley: University of California Press, 1979.

Lewis, C. S. "The Alliterative Metre." In *Rehabilitations and Other Essays*, 119–32. Oxford: Oxford University Press, 1939.

Lewis, Richard A. "Old English Poetry: Alliteration and Structural Interlace." *Language and Style* 6 (1973): 196–205.

Leyerle, John. "The Interlace Structure of *Beowulf*." *University of Toronto Quarterly* 37 (1967): 1–17.

Lowell, Robert. *Imitations.* New York: Farrar, Straus and Cudahy, 1961.

Malof, Joseph. *A Manual of English Meters.* Bloomington: Indiana University Press, 1970.

Mathews, Jackson. "Third Thoughts on Translating Poetry." In *On Translation*, edited by Reuben Brower, 67–77. Cambridge: Harvard University Press, 1959.

Morgan, Edwin, trans. *Beowulf.* Berkeley: University of California Press, 1964.

Nabokov, Vladimir. "The Servile Path." In *On Translation*, edited by Reuben Brower, 97–110. Cambridge: Harvard University Press, 1959.

Nicholson, Lewis E. "Hunlafing and the Point of the Sword." In *Anglo-Saxon Poetry: Essays in Appreciation (for John McGalliard)*, edited by Lewis E. Nicholson and Dolores W. Frese, 50–61. Notre Dame, Ind.: University of Notre Dame Press, 1975.

Norman, Frederick. "The Early Germanic Background of Old English Verse." In *Medieval Literature and Civilization: Studies in Memory of G. N. Garmonsway*, edited by D. A. Pearsall and R. A. Waldron, 3–27. London: Athlone Press, 1969.

Nowottny, Winifred. *The Language Poets Use*. London: University of London Press, 1965.

Pannwitz, Rudolph. "The Shock of the Foreign." Translated by W. S. Duell. *Delos* 4 (1970): 198–201.

Paris, Jean. "Translation and Creation." In *The Craft and Context of Translation*, edited by William Arrowsmith and Roger Shattuck, 77–91. Garden City, N.Y.: Anchor Books, 1964.

Partridge, A. C. *A Companion to Old and Middle English Studies*. London: Andre Deutsch, 1982.

Payne, F. Anne. "Three Aspects of Wyrd in *Beowulf*." In *Old English Studies in Honour of John C. Pope*, edited by Robert B. Burlin and Edward B. Irving, Jr., 15–35. Toronto: University of Toronto Press, 1974.

Paz, Octavio. *The Bow and the Lyre*. Translated by Ruth L. C. Simms. Austin: University of Texas Press, 1973. Reprint. New York: McGraw-Hill, 1975.

Pepperdene, Margaret W. "Beowulf and the Coastguard." *English Studies* 47 (1966): 409–19.

Pope, John C. *The Rhythm of Beowulf*. Rev. ed. New Haven: Yale University Press, 1968.

Quirk, Randolph. "Poetic Language and Old English Metre." In *Early English and Norse Studies: Presented to Hugh Smith in Honour of His Sixtieth Birthday*, edited by Arthur Brown and Peter Foote, 150–71. London: Methuen, 1963.

Raffel, Burton. *The Forked Tongue: A Study of the Translation Process*. The Hague: Mouton, 1971.

———, trans. *Beowulf*. Amherst: University of Massachusetts Press, 1971.

Raw, Barbara. *The Art and Background of Old English Poetry*. London: Edward Arnold, 1978.

Renoir, Alan. "Point of View and Design for Terror in *Beowulf*." *Neuphilologische Mitteilungen* 63 (1962): 154–67.

———. "The Terror of Dark Waters: A Note on Virgilian and Beowulfian Techniques." In *The Learned and the Lewed: Studies in Chaucer and Medieval Literature*, edited by Larry Benson, 147–60. Cambridge: Harvard University Press, 1974.

Robertson, D. W. "The Doctrine of Charity in Medieval Literary Gardens." *Speculum* 26 (1951): 24–49.

Robinson, Fred C. "Lexicography and Literary Criticism: A Caveat." In *Philological Essays: Studies in Old and Middle English Language and Literature in Honour of Herbert Dean Meritt*, edited by James L. Rosier, 99–110. The Hague: Mouton, 1970.

Roethke, Theodore. *On the Poet and His Craft*. Edited by Ralph J. Mills, Jr. Seattle: University of Washington Press, 1974.

Roget's International Thesaurus. 3d ed. New York: Crowell, 1962.

Rosier, James L. "Design for Treachery: The Unferth Intrigue." *PMLA* 77 (1962): 1–7.

Ryding, William W. *Structure in Medieval Narrative*. De proprietatibus litterarum, series maior, no. 12. The Hague: Mouton, 1971.

Savory, Theodore. *The Art of Translation*. London: Jonathan Cape, 1957.

Shippey, T. A. *Beowulf*. London: Edward Arnold, 1978.

——. *Poems of Wisdom and Learning in Old English*. Cambridge: D. S. Brewer, 1976.

Sievers, Eduard. "Old Germanic Metrics and Old English Metrics." In *Essential Articles for the Study of Old English*, edited by Jess B. Bessinger, Jr. and Stanley J. Kahrl, 267–88. Hamden, Conn.: Archon Books, 1968.

Stanley, E. G. "Old English Poetic Diction and the Interpretation of 'The Wanderer,' 'The Seafarer,' and 'The Penitent's Prayer.'" *Anglia* 73 (1956): 413–66.

——. "Two Old English Poetic Phrases Insufficiently Understood for Literary Criticism: Ðing Gehegan and Seonoð Gehegan." In *Old English Poetry*, edited by Daniel G. Calder, 67–90. Berkeley: University of California Press, 1979.

Steiner, George. *After Babel*. New York: Oxford University Press, 1977.

Stenton, Frank. *Anglo-Saxon England*. 3d ed. Oxford: Clarendon Press, 1971.

Stevick, Robert D. "Christian Elements and the Genesis of *Beowulf*." *Modern Philology* 61 (1963–64): 79–89.

Stjerna, Knut, *Essays on Questions Connected with the Old English Poem of Beowulf*. Translated and edited by John R. Clark Hall. Coventry: Curtis and Beamish, 1912.

Sullivan, J. P. *Ezra Pound and Sextus Propertius*. Austin: University of Texas Press, 1964.

Thomas, Dylan. *The Collected Poems of Dylan Thomas*. New York: New Directions, 1957.

Tolkien, J. R. R. "The Homecoming of Beorhtnoth Beorhthelm's Son." In *Tree and Leaf*, 149–75. London: Unwin, 1975.

——. "The Monsters and the Critics." In *The Beowulf Poet*, edited by Donald K. Fry, 8–56. Englewood Cliffs, N.J.: Prentice-Hall, 1968.

——. Prefatory Remarks. *Beowulf*. Translated by John Clark Hall. Rev. ed. London: Allen and Unwin, 1967.

Vaughan, M. F. "A Reconsideration of 'Unferð.'" *Neuphilologische Mitteilungen* 77 (1976): 32–48.

Waterhouse, Mary, trans. *Beowulf*. Cambridge: Bowes and Bowes, 1949.

Whallon, William. "The Diction of *Beowulf*." *PMLA* 76 (1961): 309–19.

Whitelock, Dorothy. *The Audience of Beowulf*. Oxford: Clarendon Press, 1951.

——. "The Prose of Alfred's Reign." In *Continuations and Beginnings*, edited by E. G. Stanley, 67–103. London: Thomas Nelson and Sons, 1966.

Williams, R. A. *The Finn Episode in Beowulf*. Cambridge: University Press, 1924.

Williams, William Carlos. *Selected Poems*. Edited by Randall Jarrell. New York: New Directions, 1949.

Winter, Warner. "Impossibilities of Translations." In *The Craft and Context of Translation*, edited by William Arrowsmith and Roger Shattuck, 93–112. Garden City, N.Y.: Anchor Books, 1964.

Wrenn, C. L., ed. *Beowulf*. New York: St. Martin's Press, 1973.

Wright, David, trans. *Beowulf*. Bungay: Richard Clay, 1957.

Wyld, Henry Cecil. "Diction and Imagery in Anglo-Saxon Poetry." *Essays and Studies by Members of the English Association* 11 (1925): 49–91.

——. "Experiments in Translating *Beowulf*." In *Studies in English Philology: A*

Miscellany in Honor of Frederick Klaeber, edited by Kemp Malone and Martin Ruud, 217–31. Minneapolis: University of Minnesota Press, 1929.

Yeats, W. B. *The Collected Poems of W. B. Yeats.* New York: Macmillan, 1969.

———. *Essays and Introductions.* London: Macmillan, 1973.

PALO ALTO COLLEGE LRC
1400 W. VILLARET
SAN ANTONIO, TEXAS 78224

PR 1585 .H84 1990
Hudson, Marc, 1947-
Beowulf

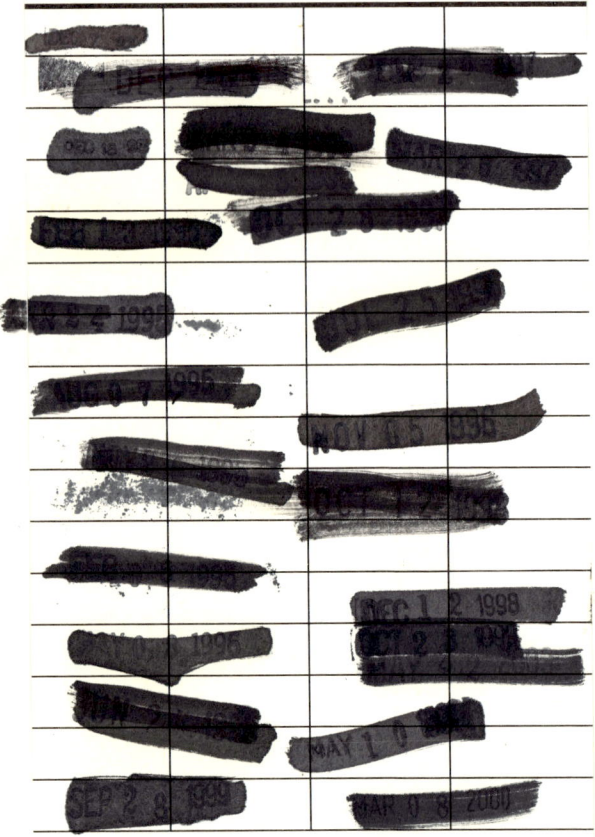

WITHDRAWN